RENAISSANCE CONCEPTS OF MAN

D1611764

*the text of this book is printed
on 100% recycled paper*

RENAISSANCE CONCEPTS OF MAN

and other Essays

PAUL OSKAR KRISTELLER

HARPER TORCHBOOKS

Harper & Row, Publishers

New York, Evanston, San Francisco, London

To Herbert Dieckmann

First HARPER TORCHBOOK edition published 1972.

LIBRARY OF CONGRESS CATALOG CARD NUMBER: 72–80869

STANDARD BOOK NUMBER: 06–138891–2

Designed by Yvette A. Vogel

CONTENTS

τέτλαθι δή, κραδίη • καὶ κύντερον ἄλλο ποτ᾽ ἔτλης

Homer, Odyssey 20,18

PREFACE

The first three essays in this small volume were delivered as Arensberg Lectures under the auspices of the Francis Bacon Foundation at the Claremont Graduate School and University Center on May 17, 19, and 21, 1965. I am grateful to Mrs. Elizabeth S. Wrigley, president of the Francis Bacon Foundation in Claremont, California, for her generous initiative in having these lectures delivered and finally published and to Professor Frederick Sontag of the Claremont Graduate School for his invitation and subsequent interest. The first essay has also been given as a separate lecture at different times at Columbia University, at the University of Chicago, at Wheaton College, at the University of North Carolina, at Harvard University, at Smith College, and at the University of California at Davis.

The two subsequent essays were delivered at the Fondazione Giorgio Cini in Venice on September 13 and 14, 1963 at the invitation of Professor Vittore Branca and published in Italian without footnotes in the volume *Venezia e l'Oriente fra Tardo Medioevo e Rinascimento* (edited by Agostino Pertusi [Florence: Sansoni, 1966], pp. 19–33 and 103–116). The first of these two essays was also printed in Italian with footnotes in *Lettere Italiane*

(16 [1964]: 1–14). The second was delivered as a lecture at the University of California at Los Angeles on May 20, 1965. Both essays appear here for the first time in English, and the second appears for the first time with footnotes.

The sixth essay was delivered as the Wimmer Lecture at St. Vincent College, Latrobe, Pennsylvania on October 25, 1961, and was published in a separate volume as Wimmer Lecture XV by the Archabbey Press in 1966. It was also delivered as a lecture at different times at Bryn Mawr College and the University of Chicago, before the Medieval Club of New York, and before the New York Philosophy Club.

The last essay appeared in the *Journal of the History of Philosophy* (Vol. II, No. 1 [April, 19, 1964], pp. 1–14).

I wish to thank Professor Vittore Branca, the editors of the Archabbey Press and Professor Richard H. Popkin for their permission to reprint the essays first printed under their auspices.

The first three essays were written as a unit and attempt to trace three major themes in Renaissance thought, unlike my other papers and lectures that usually deal with individual thinkers or currents of the period. The second three essays, in describing the Byzantine and medieval backgrounds of Renaissance thought, offer a supplement to my first Torchbook, *Renaissance Thought* (1961) in which the classical sources of Renaissance thought are discussed. The last essay is entirely methodological in nature and is here given as an appendix to illustrate my view of the field in which I have been working and to which these essays all belong.

I wish to thank Mr. Hugh Van Dusen, my editor and old friend, for his help and advice in planning and putting together this volume. I must take the blame for the long delay that has occurred between the delivery and the publication of the Arensberg Lectures.

Paul Oskar Kristeller

New York, Columbia University
March 28, 1972

I Renaissance Concepts of Man
The Arensberg Lectures

1. The Dignity of Man

If we think or hear of such a topic as "renaissance concepts of man," we are immediately reminded of a view of the Renaissance period that is widespread and has often been repeated: the Renaissance, according to this view, had a special interest in, and concern with, man and his problems. Very often, and in my view mistakenly, this notion is associated with the phenomenon called Renaissance humanism, and in stressing the difference which distinguishes the Renaissance from the period preceding it, it has been pointedly asserted that the thought of the Renaissance was man-centered, whereas medieval thought was God-centered. Many historians have praised the Renaissance for this so-called humanistic tendency and have seen in it the first step in an intellectual development that was to lead toward the Enlightenment and toward modern secular thought. Other historians, more sympathetic to the Middle Ages and less enthusiastic about modern secular thought, have held the same factual view while reversing the value judgment, stating, as one of them put it, that the Renaissance was the Middle Ages minus God.[1]

1. E. Gilson, *Les idées et les lettres,* 2d ed. (Paris, 1955), p. 192.

Yet the view of the Renaissance which we have indicated is subject to certain difficulties and, hence, has often been questioned in recent years. On the one hand, it is quite clear that the emphasis which Renaissance thought placed on man, and the manner in which it conceived of his place in the world, was not entirely new and that similar views can be found in ancient and medieval writers, views which in some instances were demonstrably known to Renaissance thinkers and even cited or used by them.[2] On the other hand, Renaissance thought, when seen in its entire range, say, from 1350 to 1600, presents a very complex picture. Different schools and thinkers expressed a great variety of views, on problems related to the conception of man as on others, and it would be extremely difficult if not impossible to reduce all of them to a single common denominator.

In spite of these difficulties, I believe that there is at least a core of truth in the view that Renaissance thought was more "human" and more secular, although not necessarily less religious, than medieval thought and that it was more concerned with human problems—a tendency that has recently been branded as antiscientific by some historians of science. But when we try to answer the question of what the Renaissance concept of man really was, we face several grave difficulties. Not only do we have to consider a great variety of views on the same problem, but the problem itself is far too broad and complex to permit any simple answer. One of the secrets of the so-called scientific method, which applies not only to the disciplines usually called sciences, but also to such fields as philosophy and history that are not commonly known by that honorific designation, consists in asking very specific questions which may permit us to find specific answers for them. Now the concept of man is not such a specific problem. It involves a great variety of moral, political, and religious questions with which we can hardly deal in these essays, let alone in this first one. The

2. E. Garin, "La 'dignitas hominis' e la letteratura patristica," *La Rinascita* Vol. I, No. 4 (1938), pp. 102–146.

problems of free will, fate, and predestination are in a broad sense human problems that are intimately connected with the concept of man, and these problems were widely discussed by the thinkers of the Renaissance and of the Reformation. The theological doctrine of sin and salvation is, broadly speaking, a human question, and it was no less debated during the Renaissance than during the Middle Ages; or even more so, if we consider the Reformation of the sixteenth century as a part of the Renaissance period. Another distinctly human problem is the more or less optimistic or pessimistic view of life held by Renaissance writers, a problem that has been treated by several scholars. Whereas the older view tended to describe the Renaissance as an optimistic age, Professor Trinkaus has shown us how deep and widespread a pessimistic view of life was present even among the leading humanists of the period, and more recently Professor Garin has pointedly asserted that the Renaissance was a splendid but not a happy age.[3]

All these questions, and a number of others, are rather important and quite relevant to our topic, but they are far too broad and complex for a short discussion such as this. Instead, we shall focus attention on three specific problems related to this topic—that is, the dignity of man, the immortality of the soul, and the unity of truth—and shall limit discussion on the whole to the thought of a few specific thinkers whom I happen to know best, but whom I should like to consider sufficiently important and influential to justify their selection.

In discussing the Renaissance notion of man's dignity and of his place in the universe, we shall treat mainly the views of Petrarch, Ficino, Pico and Pomponazzi, four authors who together may be

3. This remark was made in a lecture, and to my knowledge has not been printed. For the whole subject of this paper, see G. Gentile, "Il concetto dell'uomo nel Rinascimento," in his *Il pensiero italiano del Rinascimento,* 3d ed. (Florence, 1940), pp. 47–113; E. Garin, *Der italienische Humanismus* (Bern, 1947); Charles E. Trinkaus, *Adversity's Noblemen: The Italian Humanists on Happiness* (New York, 1940, repr. 1965); G. Saitta, *Il pensiero italiano nell' umanesimo e nel rinascimento,* Vol. I (Bologna, 1949).

considered representative of the early Italian Renaissance, if not of
the entire period or of all Europe and who have at least this much
in common that they do assign an important place to man in their
scheme of things.[4] These are by no means the only voices that
have come down to us from the period. Many important thinkers
seem to pay much less attention to this particular problem, and
others, even among the Italians, would express quite different
views on the matter. To the doctrines which we are going to discuss we may not only oppose those of Luther or Calvin, who insist
on the depravity of man after Adam's fall, perhaps in conscious
reaction against the humanist emphasis on his dignity, but also
Montaigne who stresses man's weakness and the modest place he
occupies in the universe, and who is yet, in many other respects, a
typical representative of Renaissance humanism.[5] In other words,
the glorification of man, which we are going to discuss, was not
approved by all Renaissance thinkers, but only by some of them.

This glorification of man was by no means a new discovery of
the Renaissance. The praise of man as inventor of the arts is
common in Greek literature where the myth of Prometheus and the
second chorus of Sophocles' *Antigone* may be cited as famous
examples. The notion of man as a lesser world, a microcosm, is
widespread in the popular thought of late antiquity, and the phrase
that man is a great miracle which occurs in one of the so-called
Hermetic treatises, was eagerly cited by Pico and other Renaissance thinkers.[6] In a way classical Greek thought might be called
man-centered. This is what Cicero meant when he said of Socrates

4. For many of the texts discussed in this lecture, see the English translations and notes in *The Renaissance Philosophy of Man,* ed. E. Cassirer,
P. O. Kristeller, and J. H. Randall, Jr. (Chicago, 1948).

5. *Apologie de Raimond Sebond* (Essais II, 12), in *Essais,* ed. J. Plattard,
Vol. 2, pt. 1 (Paris, 1947), pp. 168ff. and *passim.* Cf. Donald M. Frame,
Montaigne's Discovery of Man (New York, 1955), pp. 62–73, 104–105.

6. "magnum miraculum est homo . . ." (*Asclepius* 6, in *Corpus Hermeticum,* ed. A. D. Nock and A.-J. Festugière, Vol. 2 [Paris, 1945], pp.
301–302). Cf. G. Pico della Mirandola, *De hominis dignitate,* . . . ed. E.
Garin (Florence, 1942), p. 102.

that he brought philosophy down from heaven to earth.[7] Man and his soul, his excellence and ultimate happiness occupy a central place in the philosophy of Plato and of Aristotle. Plato actually placed the human soul in the middle between the corporeal world and the transcendent world of pure forms,[8] and this notion was to be adopted and further developed by the Neoplatonists and by many medieval thinkers. The early Stoics treated the universe as a community of gods and men, and this view, as well as their notions of natural law and of the solidarity of mankind, had a wide influence on later thought through Cicero and the Roman jurists, the Neoplatonists, and St. Augustine.

On the other hand, the superiority of man over other creatures is clearly indicated in Genesis and in several other passages of the Old Testament, whereas early Christian thought with its emphasis on the salvation of mankind and on the incarnation of Christ gave at least implicit recognition to man's dignity. This notion was further developed by some of the Church Fathers, especially Lactantius and Augustine. In the medieval Christian tradition in which all these ideas were repeated and developed, the dignity of man rested primarily on his status as a creature made in the image of God and capable of attaining salvation, and less on his worth as a natural being. This natural work was often recognized in terms suggested by ancient philosophy, but no medieval thinker could avoid stressing the fact that man, on account of Adam's fall, had lost much of his natural dignity. In many ways a pessimistic view of man and his state is typical of medieval thought. The treatise on the contempt of the world by Lotharius (who was to become one of the most powerful popes, Innocent III) is not only a good example of this outlook, but also an influential one.[9] It seems

7. Cf. *Academica Posteriora,* I, 4, 15 ("a rebus occultis. . . . ad vitam communem").
8. *Timaeus* 34 b ff.
9. Lotharii Cardinalis (Innocentii III) *De miseria humane conditionis,* M. Maccarrone, ed. (Lugano, 1955). Cf. *Two Views of Man,* trans. by B. Murchland (New York, 1966), pp 1–60.

significant that the humanists Facio and Manetti wrote their treatises on the dignity and excellence of man as supplements or as criticisms of Innocent III, drawing for their arguments not only on classical sources such as Cicero, but also on the Church Fathers, especially Lactantius.[10]

In spite of these earlier precedents, we cannot escape the impression that after the beginnings of Renaissance humanism, the emphasis on man and his dignity becomes more persistent, more exclusive, and ultimately more systematic than it had ever been during the preceding centuries and even during classical antiquity. Petrarch, who in his unsystematic way so often expresses ideas which were to be elaborated by his successors, seems to have led the way in this respect also. In his treatise on his own and other people's ignorance, Petrarch stresses the point that our knowledge of nature and of the animals, even if true, is useless unless we also know the nature of man, the end for which we are born, whence we come and where we go.[11] And when he describes in a famous letter his climbing of Mont Ventoux, he tells us that overwhelmed by the marvelous view, he took his copy of Augustine's *Confessions* out of his pocket, opened it at random, and came upon the following passage: "Men go to admire the heights of mountains, the great floods of the sea, the courses of rivers, the shores of the ocean, and the orbits of the stars, and neglect themselves." "I was

10. In his preface Innocent III states that he may in a future work describe the dignity of human nature (Maccarrone, ed., p. 3). Bartholomaeus Facius states at the beginning of his treatise that he is writing about the excellence of man since Pope Innocent had not carried out his promise to write about the subject (Bartholomaei Faccii *de excellentia ac prestantia hominis. . . liber*, in Felinus Sandeus, *De rebus Siciliae epitome*, ed. M. Freherus (Hanau [1611], pp. 149–168, at p. 149). Giannozzo Manetti, after having discussed man's excellence according to his body, his soul, and his whole nature, cites and refutes Innocent III among the authors opposed to his own thesis (Janocius de Manectis, *De dignitate et excellentia hominis libri IV* [Basel, 1532], pp. 169, 183–185, 209ff.). Cf. Gentile, *Il pensiero italiano del Rinascimento*, pp. 90–113.

11. Pétrarque, *Le traité de sui ipsius et multorum ignorantia*, ed. L. M. Capelli (Paris, 1906), pp. 24–25; cf. *Renaissance Philosophy of Man*, pp. 58–59 (translation and notes by Hans Nachod).

stunned," Petrarch continues, "closed the book and was angry at myself since I was still admiring earthly things although I should have learned long ago from pagan philosophers that nothing is admirable but the soul in comparison with which, if it is great, nothing is great." Petrarch thus expressed his conviction that man and his soul are the truly important subjects of our thought, and in doing so, and this is significant, he quotes Augustine and Seneca.[12]

Later in the fourteenth century and during the fifteenth century, Renaissance scholars began to use the term "humanities" (*studia humanitatis*) for the disciplines they studied, taught, and liked. The term, borrowed from Cicero and other ancient writers, was taken up by Salutati and Bruni and came to signify, as we know from many sources, the fields of grammar, rhetoric, poetry, history, and moral philosophy.[13] The fact that the term "humanities" was applied to these subjects (and even for this there was some ancient precedent) expresses the claim that these studies are especially suitable for the education of a decent human being and, hence, are, or should be, of vital concern for man as such. By the use of this very term, the humanists expressed their basic and, as it were, professional concern for man and his dignity, and this aspiration becomes quite explicit in many of their writings. It appears as a passing notion in their orations, moral treatises, and dialogues, as we have seen in the case of Petrarch, and it even came to constitute the subject matter for some special treatises. The earliest one, written by Bartolommeo Facio, treats the subject in a strongly religious and theological context, as has been noticed by most historians.[14] What they have failed to notice is the

12. Francesco Petrarca, *Le familiari,* Vol. 1, ed. V. Rossi (Florence, 1933), p. 159; *Renaissance Philosophy of Man,* p. 44. Cf. Augustine, *Confessions X* 8.15 and Seneca, *Epistles* 8.5.
13. P. O. Kristeller, *Renaissance Thought* (New York, 1961), pp. 110 and 162.
14. See note 10. Gentile, *Il pensiero italiano del Rinascimento,* p. 92. P. O. Kristeller, "The Humanist Bartolomeo Facio and His Unknown Correspondence," in *From the Renaissance to the Counter-Reformation,*

curious fact, indicated by one of Facio's biographers many years
ago, that he was encouraged to write this treatise by a Benedictine
monk of his acquaintance, Antonio da Barga, who not only sent
Facio a letter, urging him to write a supplement to the treatise of
Pope Innocent III but even attached to his letter an outline of the
treatise, which Facio seems to have followed to a certain degree.[15]
It would be easy to draw the amusing inference from this episode
that the first humanist treatise on the dignity of man was really of
monastic, and hence of medieval inspiration. However, it would be
more correct to say that an Italian monk of the fifteenth century,
who happened to be also a friend of Manetti and of other humanists and the author of treatises that we may call humanistic, was
himself affected by the humanistic culture of his age and hence
able to make direct and indirect contributions to it.[16] More important and more substantial than Facio's treatise on the dignity of
man is the treatise composed shortly afterwards by Giannozzo
Manetti, another noted humanist famous for his philosophical and
theological interests, his biblical translations, and his Hebrew
studies whose work has not yet received sufficient scholarly attention.[17] Manetti never questions or challenges the theological
doctrines of sin and salvation or of man as an image of God, but in
his treatise on man's dignity, man is primarily praised for his
reason, for his arts and skills, on account of his natural condition,
and of his secular knowledge.

When we enter the second half of the fifteenth century, the
philosophical scene in Italy, and especially in Florence, came to be
increasingly dominated by a new Platonic current which had its
center in the so-called Florentine Academy and found expression

Essays in Honor of Garrett Mattingly, ed. Charles H. Carter (New York,
1965), pp. 56–74 at 68, 73–74.

15. Kristeller, "Facio," pp. 68 and 74.

16. See now P. O. Kristeller, "The Contribution of Religious Orders to
Renaissance Thought and Learning," *American Benedictine Review* 21
(1970): 1–55.

17. See now H. W. Wittschier, *Giannozzo Manetti* (Cologne and Graz,
1968). Cf. note 10.

in the writings of its founder Marsilio Ficino, his younger friend and associate, Giovanni Pico, and some other members of their circle. Unlike the earlier humanists, whose interests and concerns were largely literary and scholarly and whose philosophical ideas were on the whole limited to the field of moral philosophy and expressed in a loose and unsystematic fashion, Ficino and Pico, in spite of their wide knowledge and interests, were primarily professional philosophers and metaphysicians, well grounded in the texts and doctrines, terminology and methodology of ancient and medieval philosophy. Hence, I am disinclined to treat Renaissance Platonism merely as a part or offshoot of Renaissance humanism, as many historians of philosophy have done, and prefer to assign to it a distinctive place within the framework of Renaissance thought.[18] I do not wish to deny that Ficino and Pico were linked rather closely with earlier and contemporary humanism. These ties are strong, and they do not merely affect the scholarly methods and the literary style of the two thinkers, but also their historical orientation and some of their central ideas and problems. In the treatment of the problem with which we are concerned in this essay, the relation of Ficino and Pico to the earlier humanists is quite clear: they share with their humanist predecessors and take over from them a profound concern with man and his dignity; but they develop this notion within a framework that was completely absent in the earlier humanists, that is, they assign to man a distinctive position within a well-developed metaphysical system of the universe, and they define and justify man's dignity in terms of his metaphysical position.

Ficino did not dedicate a special treatise to the subject of man and his dignity, as Manetti had done, but he discusses the problem rather prominently in his major philosophical work, the *Platonic Theology,* which contains a number of striking passages on the

18. P. O. Kristeller, "Florentine Platonism and Its Relations with Humanism and Scholasticism," *Church History,* 8 (1939): 201–211; "Giovanni Pico della Mirandola and His Sources," in *L'Opera e il Pensiero di Giovanni Pico della Mirandola,* I (Florence, 1965): 35–133, at 56–57.

subject. In trying to illustrate the divinity of the human soul, Ficino describes at length man's skill in the arts and in government, as Manetti had done before him.[19] He also stresses the intermediary position of the human soul between the incorporeal and the corporeal worlds, and if I am not mistaken, he reconstructs the Neoplatonic hierarchy of being in such a way that the rational soul which stands for man comes to occupy the place in the center, below God and the angels and above qualities and bodies.[20] Moreover, Ficino insists on the universality of the human mind and sees in this its basic affinity with God. The soul tends to know all truth and to attain all goodness; it tries to become all things and is capable of living the life of all beings higher and lower. In this way the soul tries to become God, and this is its divinity.[21] It is, however, inferior to God, since God actually is all things, whereas the soul merely tends to become all things.[22] Thus centrality and universality are the chief grounds and aspects of man's excellence according to Ficino. The human soul is praised as the bond and juncture of the universe that contributes in a unique way to its unity.[23] Two other ideas which occur in Ficino are worth mentioning because they were to be developed by later thinkers more fully than by him: man is to dominate all elements and all animals, and thus is the born lord and ruler of nature,[24] and man the astronomer, who can understand the motions of the celestial spheres and construct a model of

19. *Theologia Platonica*, XIII, 3 (*Opera*, Basel, 1576), Vol. I, pp. 295–298; *Théologie Platonicienne*, Vol. 2, ed. R. Marcel (Paris, 1964), pp. 223–229. Cf. P. O. Kristeller, *The Philosophy of Marsilio Ficino* (New York, 1943), p. 119.

20. Kristeller, *Philosophy*, pp. 106–108.

21. *Theologia Platonica*, XIV, 2–5 (*Opera*, pp. 307–314; ed. Marcel, pp. 250–266).

22. *Theol. Plat.*, XIV, 3 (*Opera*, p. 309; ed. Marcel, p. 256).

23. Kristeller, *Philosophy*, p. 120.

24. *Theol. Plat.*, XIII, 3. For a comparison with Francis Bacon's notion of the dominion of man over nature, see P. O. Kristeller, "Ficino and Pomponazzi on the Place of Man in the Universe," in *Studies in Renaissance Thought and Letters* (Rome, 1956), pp. 279–286 at 285.

them on a smaller scale, is virtually endowed with a mind similar to that of God who constructed the spheres themselves.[25]

When we pass to the doctrine of man in Pico della Mirandola, we shall see that he follows in several respects the doctrine of his older friend Ficino, but Pico also modifies that doctrine in a number of significant points. Pico's treatment of the question is best known from his so-called Oration on the Dignity of Man. I say so-called, for the phrase "on the dignity of man" was not used by the author but was added only by later editors. As a matter of fact, this phrase suits only the first half of the work, whereas the other half deals with entirely different questions. The original title of the work is merely "Oration," and this title is perfectly sufficient since Pico wrote no other oration besides this one. The oration was composed in 1486 to serve as an introductory speech for a public disputation on his 900 theses that Pico planned to hold in Rome.[26] Pico wrote the speech at least in two versions, and the text of the earlier version has been recently discovered and published by Eugenio Garin.[27] This earlier version is shorter than the final one, and it contains a few striking phrases of its own but does not differ from the final version in its basic content. When a papal commission found that some of the 900 theses were heretical or subject to a heretical interpretation, Pope Innocent VIII condemned the theses and prohibited the disputation. The speech thus was never delivered, and it was never published during Pico's lifetime. However, Pico used some parts of it in a defense of his theses which he published in 1487,[28] and the original oration was printed shortly after his death in the collection of his works edited by his nephew.[29]

25. Kristeller, *Studies,* pp. 279–286; G. Gentile, *Il pensiero italiano del Rinascimento,* pp. 80–81.

26. Pico, *De hominis dignitate,* ed. Garin (1942), p. 18.

27. E. Garin, *La cultura filosofica del Rinascimento italiano* (Florence, 1961), pp. 231–240.

28. Kristeller, "Giovanni Pico," p. 53.

29. Johannes Picus, *Commentationes,* 2 vols. (Bologna, 1496; Hain 12992).

In beginning his oration, Pico takes the dignity of man as his point of departure. He starts with two quotations, one of which is the passage on man as a miracle found in the Hermetic *Asclepius* and quoted already by Ficino for the same purpose.[30] Asking what really constitutes the superiority of man over other beings, Pico rejects some traditional answers as insufficient, among them the view that man is the intermediary between stable eternity and fluid time and, as the Persians say, the bond of the world.[31] The last point evidently contains a critique of Ficino, and Pico's subsequent remarks show the reasons for this divergence. In order to explain man's position and peculiar character, Pico describes the moment of his creation. When the creation of the whole universe had been completed, the Creator decided to add a being capable of meditating on the reasons of the world, loving its beauty, and admiring its greatness. Thus He undertook the creation of man. All gifts had by then been distributed among the other creatures, Pico continues, with a clear allusion to the myth of Plato's *Protagoras*.[32] Hence, the Creator decided that the being for which nothing had been left as its peculiar property might in turn have a share of all the gifts that had first been assigned singly to the various other beings. Man, therefore, has no clearly determined essence or nature. He is neither celestial nor earthly, neither mortal nor immortal. On the contrary, he may become all of this through his own will. The Creator gave him the germs of every sort of life. Depending on whatever potentiality he develops, he may become a plant, an animal, a celestial being, an angel, or he may even be unified with God Himself.[33] Man therefore possesses all possibilities within himself. It is his task to overcome the lower forms of life and to elevate himself toward God.

---

30. G. Pico della Mirandola, *De hominis dignitate,* ed. Garin, p. 102. Ficinus, *Theol. Plat.,* XIV, 3 (*Opera,* p. 310; ed. Marcel, p. 257).

31. *De hominis dignitate,* ed. Garin, p. 102.

32. *Ibid.,* p. 104. Cf. Plato, *Protagoras,* 321 b–d.

33. *Ibid.,* p. 106.

The famous passage which we have just summarized requires some further comment. It has been argued quite often that Pico seems to attribute to man an unlimited freedom, and thus to deny, at least by implication, the Christian doctrines of grace and pre-destination. This view may easily be exaggerated, for Pico never denies these doctrines, and even in this passage we should not overlook a significant detail: the often quoted words about man's freedom are addressed by God to Adam upon his creation, that is, before his fall. Hence, we might stretch the point and insist that Pico describes man's dignity before the fall, and somehow leaves it undetermined to what extent this dignity has been affected by the fall and by original sin. Nothing in what Pico says excludes the view that man in his present state needs the help of divine grace in order to make the best choice among those that are open to him on account of his nature.

If we compare Pico's position on purely philosophical grounds with that of Ficino, it is evident that Pico follows Ficino in his insistence on man's universal nature and on his share in the gifts of all other beings. This conception is based on the ancient idea of man the microcosm, and it constitutes for Pico, as for Ficino, one of the basic reasons for man's privileged place in the universe. On the other hand, Pico differs from Ficino at the point where the latter assigns to man and his soul a central but fixed place in the universal hierarchy of things. For Pico, man has no determined nature and no fixed place in the hierarchy of beings, but he is somehow placed outside this hierarchy. This fact is closely connected with the greater emphasis Pico gives to man's freedom of choice between the different natures or ways of life all of which are equally possible for him. I should like to go even further and suggest that it was Pico's passionate concern with freedom (which is also apparent in several other aspects of his thought) which made the notion of a fixed though central position of man unacceptable to him and compelled him to place man outside the hierarchy. This is a rather bold view, and it may be considered as one of the first steps in dissolving the notion of the great chain of being that had dominated Western thought for so many centuries.[34]

Pico's position is noteworthy for one additional point. His insistence on man's freedom to choose his own nature among many potentialities does not mean that all choices are equally good or desirable. On the contrary, there is a clear order and rank among these possibilities, and it is man's task and duty to choose the highest form of life that is accessible to him. Man's dignity consists in his freedom of choice because the different possibilities open to him include the highest; his dignity is fully realized only when this highest possibility is chosen. Even if we disregard the theological background of Pico's thought and consider only his secular emphasis on man's unlimited freedom, he does not mean to suggest that human nature in any of its given forms, or human choice in any of its varieties is equally good or dignified. Pico rather thinks in terms of moral and intellectual alternatives. Man's excellence is realized only when he chooses the higher forms of moral and intellectual life that are open to him, and this excellence belongs to his given nature only in so far as this nature includes among its potentialities those higher forms of life.

One of the recent interpreters of Pico, who made a valuable contribution by exploring some of the medieval sources of Pico's thought, dismissed the Oration as a mere rhetorical exercise and believed that the doctrine of the dignity of man as it appears in the Oration is nothing but a piece of oratory and, hence, should not be taken too seriously in a philosophical account of Pico's thought.[35] I cannot agree with his view. First of all, the fact that an author

34. For the history of this notion, see A. E. Lovejoy, *The Great Chain of Being* (Cambridge, Mass., 1953). For Pico, cf. E. Cassirer, *Individuum und Kosmos in der Philosophie der Renaissance* (Darmstadt, 1963), pp. 88–90; *The Individual and the Cosmos in Renaissance Philosophy,* trans. by M. Domandi [New York, 1963], pp. 84–85).

35. Avery Dulles, *Princeps Concordiae: Pico della Mirandola and the Scholastic Tradition* (Cambridge, Mass., 1941), pp. 15–16.

uses the genre of the oration in presenting some of his ideas does not prove in itself that he fails to believe in the validity of these ideas. It is certainly true that an orator will adapt his words and thoughts to a given occasion. But the question whether a particular piece of oratory does or does not reflect the considered thought of its author must be examined in each case on the basis of available evidence, and the answer will vary according to the character of the author and of the oration that are being examined. Pico was not the kind of rhetorician who would readily lend emphatic expression to ideas which he did not believe in. The very care he took in writing and revising his speech and the way in which he refers to it in his letters tend to prove, on the contrary, that he felt very strongly about the ideas contained in it.

Moreover, there is an even stronger argument against a merely rhetorical interpretation of the speech and in favor of its positive philosophical meaning. Several of the main ideas contained in the Oration are repeated by Pico in other works which cannot be dismissed as rhetorical. For example, the idea which dominates the second part of the Oration, that is, that the opposed views of different philosophical schools may be reconciled and that there is some truth in the teachings of all major philosophers and theologians, is repeated verbatim in the *Apologia,* the treatise with which Pico tried to defend his theses against the charges of the papal commission and which is otherwise quite doctrinal and even scholastic in its style and character.[36] And the doctrine of the dignity of man which occupies the center of attention in the first part of the speech is repeated, at least in some of its features, in one of Pico's main doctrinal works, the *Heptaplus,* a commentary on the first section of Genesis, which he wrote and published in 1489. In this work Pico begins his exposition by distinguishing three different worlds—the elementary, the celestial, and the invisible—which form a kind of ascending hierarchy of being and constitute together, as it were, the universe of things. After having

36. See note 28.

discussed this hierarchy of three worlds, Pico introduces man as a
fourth part of the world, thus indicating once more that man does
not occupy a fixed place in the hierarchy of things, but, rather, a
place of his own outside that hierarchy.[37] In discussing the relation between these different worlds, Pico says explicitly that man is
the connection and juncture of the three other worlds and thus
echoes to some extent Ficino's notion of man as a center of the
universe and as the intermediary between the other parts of the
world.[38] Pico continues, and here he obviously refers to the
Oration, that God after the creation of the world placed man as
His image in the center of that world, just as a prince places his
monument in the center of a newly built city, where it may be seen
by all the people.[39] The question of what the dignity of man is
based on and what his affinity with God consists in occurs again,
and it is answered in terms which differ but slightly from those of
the Oration. Emphasis is given to the fact that man combines and
unites all things, not only through his thought, but also in reality
(*re ipsa*). He shares this power with God alone, and the only
difference is that God contains all things because He is the cause
of all, and man combines all things because he is the center of
all.[40] Pico then describes in detail how man contains all sub-
stances: his body corresponds to the animals, and so forth.[41] This
enumeration is very similar to the text of the Oration, and Pico
concludes it with the same quotation from the Hermetic *Asclepius,*
which we encountered already in Ficino and in the Oration.[42]
Thus, there is a close relationship between the passage in Pico's
Oration from which we started and a passage in one of his later
doctrinal works, and apart from minor differences mainly of
emphasis, the relationship is close enough to prove that the

37. *De hominis dignitate,* ed. Garin, pp. 266–268.
38. *Ibid.,* p. 300.
39. *Ibid.,* pp. 300–302.
40. *Ibid.,* p. 302.
41. *Ibid.,* p. 304.
42. *Ibid.*

passage in the Oration, in spite of its eloquence, must be taken to express Pico's considered opinion. It is one of the most famous and influential passages in Renaissance literature, and there is no reason whatsoever to minimize its significance as a representative document of Renaissance thought.

The last philosopher whom we shall consider in this essay, Pietro Pomponazzi, belongs to an entirely different intellectual tradition. He was trained at Padua and taught philosophy at that university and later at Bologna. He belongs to the professional tradition of scholastic Aristotelianism that had been identified with the European universities ever since their origin in the twelfth and thirteenth centuries.[43] The professional philosophers of this school were engaged in the detailed interpretation of the writings of Aristotle, basing themselves on Latin translations of the text and on earlier Greek, Arabic, and Latin commentaries and applying to the text a logical rather than a philological or historical method. Being interested in the subject matter of logic and physics, and to a lesser extent of ethics and metaphysics, these philosophers carried on the development of logic and of physical science during the later Middle Ages. For a long time they remained untouched by Renaissance humanism which began as a literary, scholarly, and ethical movement and was from its start strongly opposed to the scholasticism of the Aristotelians. For the understanding of Renaissance thought, Pomponazzi is important because he shows that the Aristotelian tradition remained strong and vigorous in spite of the humanist attacks directed against it. At the same time it is significant to see that Pomponazzi, without ever abandoning the Aristotelian tradition, was affected in an indirect way by the new currents of humanism and Platonism. This latter fact becomes quite apparent when we focus our attention on his conception of man's dignity and his place in the universe.

43. J. H. Randall, Jr., *The School of Padua and the Emergence of Modern Science* (Padua, 1961); P. O. Kristeller, "Renaissance Aristotelianism," *Greek, Roman and Byzantine Studies,* 6 (1965): 157–174.

I shall largely limit my discussion of Pomponazzi to his famous treatise on the immortality of the soul which was published in 1516 and immediately became the subject of a heated controversy among philosophers and theologians. Pomponazzi holds a "naturalistic" view of the human soul and does not believe that its immortality can be proven on rational grounds, as we shall see in the second essay. Nevertheless, he endorses the traditional medieval and Neoplatonic doctrine that the human soul occupies a middle position in the universe, and he formulates this notion in terms that are quite reminiscent of Ficino and of Pico. "Man is not of simple but of multiple, not of a fixed, but of an ambiguous nature, and he is placed in the middle between mortal and immortal things. . . Hence the ancients rightly placed him between eternal and temporal things, since he is neither purely eternal nor purely temporal, because he participates in both natures. Thus existing in the middle, he has the power to assume either nature."[44] Man occupies an intermediary place between the pure intelligences of the angels and the irrational souls of the animals. Yet, whereas the Platonists had taught that the goal of human life is contemplation and that this goal is fully attained only in a future life, Pomponazzi formulates the ideal of a moral virtue which can be attained during the present life. In this manner the dignity of man is not merely maintained, but man's present earthly life is credited with an intrinsic significance that does not depend on any hopes or fears for the future. The peculiar excellence of man consists in his moral virtue, according to Pomponazzi, and this excellence can and should be attained by every person, whereas contemplation is attainable only for a few privileged persons.[45] This view of human life is the more remarkable since it is at variance with the position held by Aristotle in his *Nicomachean*

44. Petrus Pomponatius, *Tractatus de immortalitate animae*, ch. 1, ed. G. Morra (Bologna, 1954), p. 38; *Renaissance Philosophy of Man*, p. 282.
45. *Ibid.* ch. 14, pp. 184–204; *Renaissance Philosophy of Man*, pp. 353–363.

Ethics and elsewhere. In concise statements that are reminiscent of Plato and the Stoics, rather than of Aristotle, and resemble Spinoza and Kant, Pomponazzi states that virtue is essentially its own reward, and vice, its own punishment and that a good deed done without the hope of an external reward is superior to one done with such a hope.[46]

The same notion that human virtue has its intrinsic value and that this constitutes the peculiar dignity of man, as compared with other beings, is forcefully expressed in a shorter "Question on Immortality" which Pomponazzi wrote in 1504 and which I discovered and edited some years ago. "To last for a long time does not imply perfection . . . An oak lasts for a thousand years, but for that reason it still does not have the thousandth part of that perfection which belongs to man. It is rather more perfect to be a man for one year, than to be an oak for ten thousand years."[47]

I hope it has become apparent that the Renaissance thinkers whom we have mentioned and who represent at least three different intellectual and philosophical traditions were all very much concerned with the dignity of man and with his place in the universe. The humanistic movement which in its origin was moral, scholarly, and literary rather than philosophical in a technical sense provided the general and still vague ideas and aspirations as well as the ancient source materials. The Platonists and Aristotelians, who were professional philosophers and metaphysicians with speculative interests and training, took up these vague ideas, developed them into definite philosophical doctrines, and assigned to them an important place in their elaborate metaphysical systems.

These ideas are not only interesting in their own right, but they also exercised a wide influence on later thinkers. The notion that man rules the elements and all of nature, which we find in Ficino, has something in common with Francis Bacon's concept of man's

46. *Ibid.*
47. P. O. Kristeller, "Two Unpublished Questions on the Soul of Pietro Pomponazzi," *Medievalia et Humanistica,* 8 (1955): 76–101 at 89–90.

dominion over nature that contains, as it were, the entire program of modern science and technology. Ficino's idea that man is endowed with a god-like mind because he can understand the heavenly spheres and construct them on a smaller scale has rightly been compared with Galileo's claim that man's knowledge of mathematics is different in quantity but not in kind from that of God Himself.[48] On the other hand, Pico's tendency to abandon the rigid hierarchy of being had its counterpart in Nicolaus of Cusa and was to find its fuller development in the cosmology of Bruno and in the astronomy of Kepler and Galileo. In this way some of the ideas we have discussed are linked with the main currents of modern thought and exercised at least an indirect influence on later science and philosophy.

As I stated in the beginning, the notion of the dignity of man found prominent expression in several representative thinkers of the Renaissance period, and we have tried to discuss and to understand some of the main forms of this expression, but the concept was not universally emphasized even during the Renaissance, but rather strongly opposed by some other thinkers, for example, by the reformers and by Montaigne. This fact should not cause us too much surprise. I think it would be somewhat naïve to assume that such an idea as that of the dignity of man should ever completely dominate the thought of a given period, let alone ever attain a final victory that would assure its permanent predominance over other competing ideas in the history of thought. The notion that man occupies an exalted place in the universe, and the opposite idea that he is a small and powerless creature at the mercy of far stronger divine, natural, or historical forces, are not only contrary to each other but also complementary. Both of them are too well grounded in obvious facts of human experience and, hence, supply more or less permanent themes for human thought and discourse at any time, in the Renaissance as well as in our own time as we may easily observe. These ideas will always be debated, and

48. See notes 24–25.

whether one of them is emphasized at a given moment depends very much on the mood of the period or even of an individual thinker or writer. The notion of man's dignity may be easily exaggerated, and perhaps it was exaggerated in the Renaissance by the thinkers whom we have discussed. But in our time when the notion seems to be out of fashion, and opposite ideas tend to be exaggerated, there might be some good reason for emphasizing again the dignity of man in order to restore the balance. Human thought, we might say with Hegel, always tends to move from one extreme to another before attaining a balanced synthesis. Yet, when we try to make sense out of the idea of human dignity, we should not settle for too cheap and easy a solution, as we might be tempted to do. Man's dignity is not merely something that is given him with his birth, according to Pico, but rather something he has to attain and to realize through his own effort. What is given is merely the ability to strive toward this end. We assert our dignity as human beings not simply by being what we happen to be but by choosing the best among our potentialities, by cultivating reason rather than blind feeling, and by identifying ourselves with tasks that are morally and intellectually worthwhile and that lead us beyond the narrow confines of our personal interests and ambitions.

2. The Immortality of the Soul

Among the many problems and concepts that have occupied the thinkers of the past, and especially those of the Renaissance, the doctrine of immortality seems especially remote from the discussions and concerns of our time. In spite of a widespread talk about religion and a persistent concern with death and its significance, our outlook is very much confined to the problems of this world, and we seem to worry very little about what may happen to us or to the world after we are dead. Everything is measured by the present and its needs, and the present seems to live at the expense of the past and the future. People who have ambition eagerly seek a publicity that is quickly forgotten, and the quest for everlasting fame, once a powerful incentive for political or cultural achievement, is no longer felt or, at least, no longer admitted to be a living impulse for human endeavor. The reasons for the recent disappearance of this once strong human concern would form an important and interesting subject of historical investigation but cannot detain us in this essay. I suspect that the quest for fame presupposes a firm belief in the lasting continuity of a tradition, political or religious, philosophical or cultural, of which we wish to be a part and that this belief has been undermined for many people in a variety of ways. Yet, the deep desire to extend our perspective and our aspirations beyond the short and narrow limits of our personal life has by no means disappeared, but has found expression in other forms of thought and belief that are subtler and less tangible than the compact theories of fame and immortality that were formulated in the past. And I wonder whether the widespread curiosity now felt about distant places, times, and civilizations may not be due to an instinctive desire to extend the boundaries of our personal life, as it were, by a kind of vicarious participation. Perhaps this residual feeling may enable us to grasp the significance of those strong beliefs about the future that have sustained other times and cultures. In many religions and civilizations, primitive or more advanced, the spirits of the dead are thought to continue to live and to demand the attention of their descendants, if not of strangers. The belief that our moral conduct in this life will be followed by rewards and punishments after death was until recently, and in a sense still is, an essential part of Christian doctrine, and had been held, long before the rise of Christianity, by Greek religious and philosophical teachers. And everlasting fame was an admired and frequently asserted goal of human efforts through classical antiquity and again in modern times. It is against this background, and not only from the perspective of our present indifference to eternity, that we must try to understand the speculations of Renaissance thinkers about the immortality of the soul.

As compared with the otherworldliness of the Middle Ages, the Renaissance has often been characterized as a "thisworldly" age, and not entirely without good reasons. For it is true that Renaissance writers pay much greater attention to the problems and experiences of the present life than their predecessors, and it is much easier for the modern reader to gain from their writings a concrete and almost visual impression of their daily thoughts and activities. Yet, the Renaissance was also an age in which the desire for everlasting fame was more vocal and widespread than at any

time since classical antiquity, and Jacob Burckhardt has rightly
given an important place to this cult of fame in his still suggestive
and largely valid picture of the early Italian Renaissance.[1] As in
many other instances, Renaissance humanists were prone to repeat
what the ancients had said about the desirability of lasting fame,
but they surely had a spontaneous desire to perpetuate their own
work and reputation through fame. In a sense, the humanists knew
that by their very cult of antiquity they were reviving or keeping
alive the fame of the ancients whom they admired, and they must
have hoped that through their own labors they would come to
share in the fame of the ancients and that their students and
readers and successors would do for their own fame what they
themselves had done for that of the ancients. In dedicating their
works to the princes and notables of their time, and in carrying out
their commissions, the writers and artists of the Renaissance
thought they were insuring the fame of their patrons, and it is quite
evident that the patronage extended to the arts and to learning
during the Renaissance was partly motivated by this hope for fame
and that in some, though by no means in all instances, this hope
has been fulfilled by the judgment of posterity. The cult of fame
was linked with the belief in the dignity of man and certainly with
the pervasive individualism of the period, a phenomenon admirably described by Burckhardt and often misunderstood by his
critics.[2] When we speak about Renaissance individualism, we do
not mean the actual presence of great individuals who may be
found at any period of history, or the metaphysical emphasis on
individual objects as against universals, as we find it in nominalism, which applies to stones no less than to human beings and,
hence, is as far removed from "humanism" as is the so-called
existentialism of Thomas Aquinas from that of Kierkegaard and
his successors. We rather mean the importance attached to the

1. J. Burckhardt, *Die Kultur der Renaissance in Italien,* 13th ed. (Stuttgart, 1922), section 2, ch. 3, pp. 106–115.
2. *Ibid.,* section 2, pp. 97–126.

personal experiences, thoughts, and opinions of an individual person, and the eager or, if you wish, uninhibited expression given to them in the literature and art of the period. Behind the endless display of gossip and invective, of description and subtle reflection there is the firm belief that the personal experience of the individual writer is worth recording for the future, preserving his fame and, as it were, prolonging his life. And I cannot help feeling that the widespread and prominent concern of Renaissance thinkers with the immortality of the soul was on the metaphysical level another expression of the same kind of individualism. For in his immortal soul, the individual person continues to live more effectively than in his fame and to extend his experience into eternity. The concern for immortality and the concern for fame are effectively combined in Dante's great poem which in this way proves to be a creation, not of the high Middle Ages, but of the period of transition from the Middle Ages to the Renaissance. Because the immortality of the soul was felt to be a metaphysical projection of that individual life and experience which was the center of attention for Renaissance writers and scholars, we can understand why this doctrine, though often expressed in other times and contexts, attained in the Renaissance a greater philosophical prominence than it had at any earlier or later period and why the discussion of this problem became one of the most important and characteristic themes of Renaissance philosophy.[3] There is also a conscious link between the immortality of the soul and the dignity of man. More than once Ficino stresses the fact that the immortality of the soul is an essential part of its dignity and divinity, and he argues suggestively that without the immortality of his soul man would be inferior to the animals.[4] In the earliest

---

3. G. Di Napoli, *L'immortalità dell'anima nel Rinascimento* (Turin, 1963); E. Garin, *La cultura filosofica,* pp. 93–126; P. O. Kristeller, "Pier Candido Decembrio and His Unpublished Treatise on the Immortality of the Soul," in *The Classical Tradition: Literary and Historical Studies in Honor of Harry Caplan,* ed. L. Wallach (Ithaca, 1966), pp. 536–558.

4. Kristeller, *Philosophy of Ficino,* pp. 344–345.

humanist treatise on the dignity of man, that of Bartolommeo
Facio, the immortality of the soul is even presented as the chief
argument for man's excellence.[5] But unlike the dignity of man and
the other notions which we have just discussed, the immortality of
the soul became a prominent topic of philosophical discussion
during the fifteenth and sixteenth centuries.

As in many other instances, the Renaissance discussion of
immortality depended in many ways on ancient and medieval
sources, and the novel and distinctive traits of that discussion must
be sought in matters of detail and of emphasis. In order to understand the issues, it is necessary not merely to enumerate previous
doctrines that are roughly relevant to the problem under discussion, but also to pay attention to some precise distinctions. In
Greek popular and religious thought, as expressed by Homer, there
was something called the soul which survived as a shadow after the
death of the body, but it did not possess a life or substance that
would give it an immortality comparable to that of the gods.[6] In a
later phase of Greek religion that is associated with the name of
Orpheus, the soul was capable of religious and moral purification
and was subject to rewards and punishments after death. Among
the early philosophers the soul was mainly conceived as the animating principle of the body. It was Plato who in a sense combined the religious and philosophical notions of the soul, conceiv-
ing it both as the animating principle of the body and as a moral
and metaphysical agent capable of more or less perfect moral
status. In his myths which have been connected with Orphic
sources, Plato describes the rewards and punishments of the soul
after death and also accepts the transmigration of the soul into
other human and animal bodies as taught by the Pythagoreans. In
the doctrinal sections of his dialogues, and especially in the
Phaedo, Plato asserts and tries to demonstrate the immortality of
the soul. He conceives this immortality as the natural attribute of

5. Kristeller, "Facio," p. 68.
6. E. Rohde, *Psyche,* 2d ed. (Freiburg, 1898).

an incorporeal substance that extends into the past as well as into the future. Among his chief arguments appears that from affinity. The soul is capable of knowing the pure intelligible forms or ideas; hence, it must be incorporeal and eternal like them.[7] This Platonic doctrine of immortality was preserved and further developed by Plato's pupils and followers, and especially by the Neoplatonists. For them, not only the natural immortality of the soul as an incorporeal substance is an accepted doctrine confirmed by further arguments, but also the mythical notions of the rewards, punishments, and transmigration of the soul assume a literal significance and are made an integral part of the metaphysical system.[8] This position is not shared by the other leading schools of later Greek philosophy. Aristotle in his early writings seems to have followed Plato, but in his extant works his attitude towards immortality is, at least, ambiguous. He nowhere asserts that the soul is immortal, and whereas he does say that the intellect is incorruptible, he does not state explicitly that this incorruptible intellect is a part of the individual human soul; and thus he left room for a wide area of debate among his followers and interpreters.[9] Some of his most important ancient commentators, such as Alexander of Aphrodisias, explicitly placed the active intellect outside the individual human soul and thus tended to consider the latter as mortal. The Stoics did not consistently uphold individual immortality. They either restricted it to the sages or denied it altogether, and the doctrine of recurrent conflagrations would limit even the immortality of the sages to the present world period. Finally the Epicureans denied immortality altogether and had the soul perish together with its body, aside from considering the soul as a corporeal substance, a doctrine also held by the Stoics.

Whereas the history of the doctrine of immortality in classical

7. Plato, *Phaedo,* esp. 76d–77a. Cf. R. L. Patterson, *Plato on Immortality* (University Park, Pa., 1965).
8. Plotinus, *Ennead* II, 2–3 and IV, 7.
9. *De anima,* III, 4–5.

antiquity is pretty clear, its vicissitudes within the religious traditions of Judaism and Christianity are far less easily described.
There has been a good deal of controversy on the matter, and I
must say that my own view differs from that of many other
scholars and may be shocking to some. It is clear that some
notions of a future life appear in the Old Testament and that the
New Testament speaks very explicitly about the kingdom of God,
eternal life, and resurrection. It is also true that body and soul are
repeatedly distinguished in the New Testament and that at least
one passage speaks of the future life of the soul.[10] However, the
writers of the Bible were no professional philosophers and had a
very slight, if any, acquaintance with Greek philosophy and its
terminology. There is an occasional, but not a consistent distinction between body and soul and no hard and fast statement that
the soul (or even God) is incorporeal, or that the soul is immortal,
let alone by nature. The majority of recent theologians have been
led to admit that there is no scriptural basis for the natural immortality of the soul,[11] and those who refused to go that far have been
forced to rely on implications or on later interpretations or on the
dubious confusion of immortality with resurrection or eternal life.
The Christian doctrine of immortality is not found in Scripture,
but in the work of the early apologists and Church Fathers, from
Justinus Martyr to St. Augustine. These writers were familiar with
Greek philosophy, as the biblical authors were not, and for them it
was as vital a task to reconcile Christian doctrine with Greek
philosophy as it is for modern theologians to reconcile it with

10. "Animam autem non possunt occidere," *Ev. Matth.* 10:28. "Qui odit
animam suam in hoc mundo, in vitam aeternam custodit eam," *Ev. Joh.*
12:25. These are the only scriptural passages cited in the Lateran decree of
1512 (see below).
11. Kristeller, "Decembrio," pp. 553–555. To the literature cited there,
we may now add: R. Heinzmann, *Die Unsterblichkeit der Seele und die
Auferstehung des Leibes, Eine problemgeschichtliche Untersuchung der
fruehscholastischen Sentenzen– und Summenliteratur von Anselm von Laon
bis Wilhelm von Auxerre* (*Beitraege zur Geschichte der Philosophie und
Theologie des Mittelalters,* 40, 3 [Münster, 1965]).

modern science. The Christian notion of the immortality of the soul, as it was finally formulated by St. Augustine, is clearly derived from that of Plato and the Neoplatonists. The soul is incorporeal and by nature immortal, and one of the chief arguments of its immortality is again its affinity with God and the eternal ideas inherent in Him which the soul is able to know.[12] Of the Neoplatonic doctrine of immortality, Augustine merely rejected what was incompatible with Christian doctrine: transmigration and preexistence. Thus modified, the concept of immortality without preexistence lost some of its consistency, and the argument from affinity, some of its force, but it became a part of standard medieval doctrine, more or less taken for granted by everybody, and especially by the followers of Augustine, but it was rarely challenged or discussed in detail.

When Aristotle instead of Plato became the chief philosophical authority in the thirteenth century, the doctrine of the immortality of the soul did not gain in prominence. Thomas Aquinas duly defends the incorruptibility and future beatitude of the rational soul, but he seems to avoid the term "immortality," and he does not attach especial importance to the subject.[13] Duns Scotus explicitly states that the traditional arguments for the immortality of the soul are weak and inconclusive and adds that the belief in resurrection and eternal life should be based on faith alone.[14] Whether also immortality is based on faith he does not state with equal clarity, and I tend to doubt it, since in his time the immortality of the soul had not yet been declared to be an article of faith. Instead the Council of Vienne declared the Aristotelian definition of the soul as form of the body to be an article of faith, a striking instance of the impact which a hundred years of Aristotelian

12. Augustine, *De immortalitate animae* and *De quantitate animae* (*Oeuvres* 1,5,2, ed. P. de Labriolle, Desclée, 1939).
13. Cf. Summa Theologiae, I q.75 a.6.
14. *Opus Oxoniense*, 4, d.43, qu.2; *Reportata Parisina* 4, d.43, q.2. S. Vanni Rovighi, *L'immortalità dell'anima nei maestri francescani del secolo XIII* (Milan, 1936), pp. 197–233, Cf. Kristeller, "Decembrio," p. 553.

speculation at Paris and elsewhere were to have even on theology
and on church dogma. The scriptural grounds for this dogma
might be even harder to find than for immortality, but this is no
serious objection when traditon and church authority are given
equal power with Scripture in establishing official doctrine.

A much more serious threat to the doctrine of immortality than
the indifference of Aquinas or the fideism of Scotus was the doctrine of the unity of the intellect taught by Averroes and his Latin
followers. In interpreting the third book of Aristotle's *De anima,*
Averroes went beyond Alexander and maintained that both the
active and the passive intellect are but one for all men and exist
outside the individual human souls, and that the latter merely
participate momentarily through their thinking faculties in this
universal intellect whenever they perform an act of knowledge.[15]
In thus asserting the immortality of the universal intellect, Averroes removed at the same time the basis for the immortality of the
individual human souls which are outside this intellect and merely
have a temporary connection with it. Averroes' authority as a
commentator on Aristotle was great, and his doctrine of the unity
of the intellect exerted a great influence on all Aristotelian philosophers of the Middle Ages and the Renaissance. While the so-
called Averroists accepted the doctrine on purely philosophical
grounds and thought it to be in accordance with Aristotle, all other
Aristotelians who did not accept it still gave it careful consideration, including Thomas Aquinas, who wrote a special treatise on
the subject in which (and this is characteristic) the issue of
immortality is not prominently discussed.[16]

If we take all these facts into consideration, we arrive at the
curious and unexpected conclusion that the doctrine of immortality did not play a major role in medieval thought, especially not

15. Averroes, *Commentarium magnum in Aristotelis de anima libros,* ed.
F. Stuart Crawford (Cambridge, Mass., 1964).
16. Thomas Aquinas, *De unitate intellectus* (in his *Opuscula philosophica,*
ed. J. Perrier, Paris, 1949, pp. 71–120; trans. and annot. by Bruno Nardi,
Florence, 1947).

during the thirteenth and fourteenth centuries when the teachings of Aristotle and his commentators tended to prevail. The central importance which the doctrine came to assume during the Renaissance thus appears in a new perspective, that is, as a conscious reaction against later medieval thought, a reaction that would quite properly claim to be a fight in the name of Plato (and of Augustine) against Aristotle or, at least, against his commentators. The link between immortality and some other favorite notions of Renaissance thought might actually have been a factor in the growing vogue and appeal of Plato that we may observe from the fourteenth to the sixteenth centuries.

It has often been thought that the prominence of immortality in the Renaissance is due to the activity of the Florentine Academy and of its leader Marsilio Ficino. Yet, while it is true that Ficino was responsible for the full philosophical development of the doctrine and for much of its subsequent diffusion, we have learned more recently that the concern for immortality, just as the interest in Plato, predated the rise of Florentine Platonism. Attention has been called to a sizable number of special treatises on the immortality of the soul written by many more- or less-known humanists and theologians of the fifteenth century.[17] They greatly vary in length and diffusion and also in their sources, the orientation of their thought, and the quality of their reasoning. These treatises do not represent a unified group, and their authors do not form a school. While it is still too early to assess the contribution of these treatises, some of which have not yet been analyzed or even edited, their very existence and number prove the fact that the problem was of considerable interest at the time, as it had not been during the preceding period. Among the authors we find eclectic humanists like Pier Candido Decembrio, who relies heavily on a twelfth-century treatise attributed to St. Augustine, or Agostino Dati; humanist theologians like Antonio degli Agli, who in his treatise does not yet betray the influence of Ficino to whose circle he later

17. See above, note 3.

belonged; and Franciscan and Dominican friars such as John of
Ferrara, Philippus de Barberiis, and above all, Jacopo Camfora,
who wrote a treatise in the vernacular that had a considerable
diffusion in both manuscripts and printed editions.

This literature is significant because it indicates a background
and a climate of opinion that was receptive for a detailed discussion of the immortality of the soul such as we encounter it in the
work of Marsilio Ficino. His major philosophical work, which
consists of eighteen books and is entitled *Theologia Platonica de
immortalitate animorum,* deals mainly with the problem of immortality and might be described as a *Summa* on the immortality of
the soul.[18] Whereas the first four books deal with the hierarchy of
being, the attributes of God, and the distribution of the souls in the
universe, thus providing a general metaphysical background for the
discussion, the remainder of the work consists technically of a
series of arguments for immortality, although there are many
digressions, and many arguments serve as an occasion, and perhaps as a pretext, for discussing other philosophical problems that
are intrinsically important apart from their close or remote connection with immortality. While drawing freely on the arguments
formulated by Plato, Plotinus, Augustine, and other thinkers,
Ficino adds many of his own and also revises and recombines the
thoughts derived from his predecessors. And while it is true that in
his presentation of the doctrine he bases himself on a long and
venerable tradition and that in dedicating a special treatise to the
problem he has the precedent of some of his favorite predecessors,
it is also worth noticing that Ficino's *Platonic Theology* greatly
exceeds the immortality treatises of Plato, Plotinus, Augustine, or
other writers, both in its bulk and in the relative importance it has
within the framework of his own work and thought. Ficino became
in a sense the philosopher of immortality, and it is legitimate to
ask not only what he had to say about the subject, but also why it
came to occupy such a place in his doctrine. Such questions are

18. Kristeller, *Ficino,* p. 346.

always difficult to answer, especially in a short discussion like this. But we have indicated as one factor that the problem was of wide interest to other writers and thinkers of the fifteenth century. Other factors must be considered that are connected with Ficino's own thought and orientation. I do not think that Ficino focused from the very beginning on the problem of immortality, if we may judge his development from his preserved early writings. His prevalent interest in the problem seems to begin with the *Platonic Theology,* a work which he first composed between 1469 and 1474 and published in 1482. His intent may have been in part polemical. He was dissatisfied with the tendency of contemporary Aristotelians to separate philosophy and theology, and he considered it his task to establish a basic harmony between the two, that is, between Platonism and Christianity. He was convinced that the Averroist doctrine of the unity of the intellect undermined the immortality of the soul and thus the whole of Christian theology, since he thought, though perhaps wrongly, as many theologians before and after him, that the immortality of the soul was a pillar of Christian theological doctrine. Important for this polemical purpose of the work is the fifteenth book, which consists entirely of a series of arguments against the unity of the intellect. It is the most detailed refutation of Averroism after that of Aquinas, and a close comparison between them might lead to interesting conclusions. However, Ficino's critique was concerned primarily, and even exclusively, with the defense of immortality, as that of Thomas had not been.

Aside from this negative consideration, there are also positive elements in Ficino's thought that may explain his prevalent concern with immortality. As some of his humanist predecessors, he clearly links immortality with the divinity of the soul and of man. Even more crucial, in my opinion, is another factor. Ficino's entire analysis of man, of his life and ultimate purpose, is based on the view that the true aim of man, and especially of the philosopher, is the ascent through contemplation toward the direct vision of God.

The contemplative life is for Ficino a matter of direct spiritual experience to which he constantly points and which he actually uses as evidence for the existence of God and the divine ideas, the incorporeality and divinity of the soul, and for the claim that the human soul was actually created with the task of knowing and attaining God through contemplation. Like some of his Neoplatonic and mystical predecessors, Ficino even hints that some privileged thinkers, perhaps even himself, were able to attain a direct vision of God during their earthly life, although but for a short moment.[19] However, this is not enough. If the human soul was created with the task of attaining God and has an inborn natural appetite for God, we must postulate, unless this appetite were thought to be vain, that a large number of human beings will attain this goal in a permanent fashion. Hence, we must posit the immortality of the soul and a future life in which it will forever attain its goal, provided it has duly prepared itself for it during the present life through moral conduct, and above all, through contemplation.[20] This line of argument, which appears in a number of different versions, constitutes a recurrent theme throughout the *Platonic Theology* and is occasionally repeated in other works of Ficino. It is so closely linked with the central motive of Ficino's philosophy that I am inclined to consider it as the main argument that in his own mind was not only the most persuasive one, but the one that actually prompted him to undertake his great effort to prove immortality. The argument is not entirely original, and some of its versions may be easily traced to medieval sources or to St. Augustine, but the peculiar formulation given to it by Ficino seems to be his own, as is its predominant function and the attempt to link it with some of his other basic ideas. Aside from this argument, which we might call the argument from the natural appetite of the soul, the most important argument is that from affinity, that is, the notion that the soul is able to attain direct knowledge of

19. *Ibid.,* pp. 332 and 348.
20. *Ibid.*

incorporeal entities such as God and the ideas and must hence be itself incorporeal, incorruptible, immortal as are its objects. This argument occurs in one of its versions already in Plato, and it has been repeated throughout the Platonic and medieval tradition. It is, of course, hard to reconcile with the position of many Aristotelians who deny that the soul during the present life can know anything except sense objects. Moreover, it proves too much since it applies to preexistence as well as to future immortality, once we assume a direct present knowledge of incorporeal objects and assign to it more than an a priori meaning. Yet, Ficino considered the argument valid and made an effort to elaborate it with great detail. He could not accept preexistence any more than St. Augustine had done, but he did not attempt to demonstrate the creation of the soul as he tried to prove immortality. Rather, he seems to have considered it as an article of faith, confirmed, as it were, by one of the interpretations that may be given to Plato's *Timaeus.*

Ficino's massive work established a firm connection between the doctrine of immortality and Renaissance Platonism and also served as an arsenal of arguments for those who were interested in defending immortality on philosophical or theological grounds. The traces of its influence may be found throughout the sixteenth century and afterwards. Even in the controversy aroused by Pomponazzi to which we shall turn immediately, it is quite evident that the position identified and criticized by Pomponazzi as that of Plato is the one represented by Ficino and his *Platonic Theology,* with which Pomponazzi was clearly acquainted. On the other hand, some of Pomponazzi's opponents clearly draw on Ficino's arguments in trying to defend immortality against Pomponazzi. This is especially apparent in Agostino Nifo, as was recognized by Pomponazzi and other contemporaries,[21] and in the Augustinian hermit Ambrogio Fiandino, whose Platonic orientation and de-

---

21. Edward P. Mahoney, *The Early Psychology of Agostino Nifo,* unpublished thesis, Columbia University, 1966.

pendence on Ficino appears in a number of his other writings.[22] Historians of Averroism and of Paduan Aristotelianism are too much inclined to identify the opponents of that school in the fifteenth and sixteenth centuries with Thomism or traditional theology and fail to see or to appreciate the fact that the resistance to Averroism drew fresh strength from the humanist dislike of Aristotle, and from the Platonist critique of Averroism. It is significant that Pico della Mirandola, in his attempt to reconcile the views of different thinkers and traditions, intended to prove that the unity of the intellect was compatible with the immortality of the soul, a position that Ficino would have rejected; but we do not know the arguments with which Pico planned to defend this position.[23] The wide impact of the Platonism of the Florentine Academy on Renaissance theology appears in the writings of many sixteenth-century theologians and may even be seen in the decree by which the Lateran Council of 1512 condemned the unity of the intellect and formulated the immortality of the soul as a dogma of the Church.[24] The fact that the decree was opposed by Cajetan and that Giles of Viterbo played a prominent role at the Council tend to confirm the conclusion that this decree is as much the echo of Renaissance Platonism as the decree of Vienne about the soul as form of the body had been the echo of thirteenth-century Aristotelianism. The Lateran decree also confirms the suspicion that the immortality of the soul had to be officially promulgated as a church dogma at that late date, because it was considered indispensable for other theological doctrines but had no clear or explicit support in Scripture or other valid theological authorities. In a strict sense, the immortality of the soul as a Catholic dogma

22. He wrote commentaries on several Platonic dialogues and a defense of Plato against Georgius Trapezuntius. Cf. F. Lauchert, *Die italienischen literarischen Gegner Luthers* (Freiburg, 1912), pp. 239–240.

23. Kristeller, "Pico," p. 63.

24. J. D. Mansi, *Sacrorum Conciliorum nova et amplissima collectio,* Vol. 32 (Paris, 1902), col. 842–843. For the decree of Vienne (1311), see *ibid.,* Vol. 25 (Venice, 1782), col. 411.

owes its authority and its status as an article of faith to the Lateran decree, which is still most commonly cited by Catholic authors when they discuss the problem. When it is now so widely believed that all of our convictions, especially in ethics and metaphysics, that are not derived from modern science stem from the religious traditions of Judaism and Christianity, we may point in reply not only to the recurrent influence of Greek thought on secular philosophy and literature, but also to the numerous instances, of which the Lateran decree is but one, in which ideas first derived from Greek philosophy were actually absorbed and inextricably assimilated into the very heart of Christian, and to a lesser extent of Jewish doctrine.

A few years after the publication of the Lateran decree, the problem of immortality became again the center of philosophical and theological attention. In 1516 Pietro Pomponazzi, the Aristotelian philosopher trained at Padua and teaching at Bologna published his treatise on the immortality of the soul, in which he argues at great length that immortality cannot be demonstrated on purely natural or Aristotelian grounds, but must be accepted as an article of faith. The treatise immediately aroused violent opposition, and although Pomponazzi's opponents did not succeed in having his work officially condemned, an entire sequence of treatises was published against him, both by theologians and philosophers, including the later Cardinal Gasparo Contarini, the Augustinian hermit Ambrogio Fiandino, the Dominican Bartolommeo Spina, and the fellow Aristotelian Agostino Nifo. Pomponazzi tried to answer some of his opponents with two other works that are much longer than his original treatise—the *Apologia* and the *Defensorium*—but the controversy continued for many years, even after his death, and its repercussions may be seen as late as the eighteenth century and, if you wish, in the partisan views of many modern historians.[25]

25. Di Napoli, *L'immortalità dell'anima nel Rinascimento,* pp. 277–338; E. Gilson, "Autour de Pomponazzi," *Archives d'histoire doctrinale et*

The statement often repeated in textbooks and other popular accounts that Pomponazzi completely denied the immortality of the soul is obviously incorrect. He merely denied that it can be demonstrated on rational or Aristotelian grounds, and he even asserted that the reasons against immortality were stronger than the reasons for it but insisted that it was true as an article of faith.[26] This is what he persistently and explicitly stated, and the claim of some historians that he was not serious about it, but really meant to deny immortality altogether is merely an inference based on no textual or factual evidence. The question whether Pomponazzi was sincere in thus separating, or even opposing, reason and faith, philosophy and theology, is part of a much broader problem with which I hope to deal in my third essay. On the other hand, it has been claimed that Duns Scotus and other medieval thinkers had argued that the proofs proposed for the immortality of the soul are not valid and that hence Pomponazzi was by no means original. The answer is that Duns Scotus was far less explicit in discussing these proofs or in asserting that immortality was an article of faith and that in his time immortality had not yet been declared to be an article of faith. Moreover, Duns Scotus' remarks did not arouse much public controversy whereas Pomponazzi's did, partly on account of the Lateran decree, but also because of the much wider interest and stake Renaissance thinkers had in the problem and of the much more explicit challenge offered to it by Pomponazzi.

We have no time to go into the details of the controversy, which has received very recently much more detailed attention than in

littéraire du Moyen Age, 63 (1961, published 1962): 163–279; E. Gilson, "L'affaire de l'immortalité de l'âme à Venise au debut du XVIe siècle," in *Umanesimo europeo e umanesimo veneziano,* ed. V. Branca (Florence, 1963), pp. 31–61; Martin Pine, *Pietro Pomponazzi and the immortality controversy,* 1516–1524, unpublished thesis, Columbia University, 1965.

26. Petrus Pomponatius, *Tractatus de immortalitate animae,* ch. 15, ed. G. Morra (Bologna, 1954), pp. 232–238; *Renaissance Philosophy of Man,* pp. 377–381.

the past. I merely wish to emphasize that Pomponazzi explicitly sets his own opinions against three others which he attributes to Averroes, Plato, and Thomas Aquinas, respectively.[27] This presentation of the problem means that Pomponazzi is not merely setting up his own view against those of Averroes and St. Thomas, whom he recognizes as prominent authorities within his own Aristotelian tradition, but he also meant to deal with the Platonic position as recently restated by Marsilio Ficino whom he knows and respects. Considering the central place of immortality in Ficino's thought and the wide influence his work had exercised in this as in many other respects, we should not be surprised to see Pomponazzi offer an attack or·a counterattack against the Platonic doctrine of immortality; and the fact that he also criticizes the Thomist and Averroist position might mean that he considers them inadequate interpretations of the Aristotelian view, as against that of the Platonists. The point is of some importance because Gilson, in his recent treatment of the controversy, which is extremely subtle and fair as far as Pomponazzi is considered, interprets Pomponazzi's view exclusively against the background of Thomism and Averroism and completely ignores the Platonist position, although it had played such a prominent role in the decades preceding Pomponazzi's treatise, is explicitly discussed by Pomponazzi, and was explicitly used and restated by some, at least, of his opponents.

Pomponazzi's arguments against immortality and against the specific proofs offered in its support are numerous and complex. However, I am inclined to think that the central argument, which is often repeated in slightly different form, is the one based on the relationship of the soul to the body. The statement that the soul during the present life depends on the body, especially for its knowing activity, must be clarified by an important distinction. The statement may mean that the soul needs the body for its

27. *Ibid.*, chs. 2–8. The short discussion of Plato (chs. 5–6) is ignored by Gilson.

subject, that is, that the soul, and even the intellect, has a material substratum and may be called material in this sense. The statement may also mean that the soul needs the body for its object, that is, that it cannot attain any knowledge except through data supplied by the body through sense perception and imagination. While denying the assertion in the former sense, Pomponazzi keeps insisting on the validity of the second meaning. The result is that we have no knowledge whatsoever that is not based on bodily objects, and in this way the Platonist claim of a pure intelligible knowledge during the present life is rejected.[28] It is this claim on which the argument from affinity and also the argument from natural appetite rested, as well as the constant appeal to contemplative experience. In the claim that all human knowledge rests on sense objects, Pomponazzi goes beyond the position of Aristotle, but we still may say that his basic argument against the proofs for immortality reflects the Aristotelian position, interpreted in an empiricist or naturalist sense, as against the basic Platonist position represented by Ficino. This confrontation between Pomponazzi's Aristotelianism and Ficino's Platonism as expressed in their discussion of immortality is very instructive, and it also throws much light on the subsequent controversy, in addition to the fact that Pomponazzi, within the Aristotelian tradition, tends to criticize the interpretations offered by Averroes and by Thomas.

It might be argued that Pomponazzi's attempt to refute immortality, at least on purely natural and philosophical grounds, would show an indifference to immortality on his part and thus throw doubt on our initial claim that the problem of immortality occupied a central position in Renaissance thought. I do not think that this argument is valid. First of all, the strong and widespread reaction to Pomponazzi's treatise is sufficient to show that the problem remained at the center of philosophical and theological attention during the first half of the sixteenth century. Second, the fact that Pomponazzi devoted three of his chief works, not to

28. *Ibid.*, ch. 4.

mention an early question, to the problem of immortality shows that he is seriously concerned with it, and the fact that he arrives at the conclusion that it cannot be demonstrated merely indicates the great honesty of his thought, which appears also in his other writings. Finally, and this seems to me most important, Pomponazzi does not reject immortality altogether, even within the realm of philosophy, but holds on to a limited concept of immortality, while admitting that the more comprehensive traditional concept is philosophically untenable. In beginning his treatise, he asserts in a manner reminiscent of the Platonists that man occupies an intermediary position between mortal and immortal things, and shares through the faculties of his soul both in mortality and immortality.[29] And in the course of his work, where he formulates his own position as distinct from that of Plato, Averroes, and Thomas, he states that man is absolutely speaking (*simpliciter*) mortal, but relatively speaking (*secundum quid*) immortal, and in defending this view he states that the human intellect, though mortal, participates in immortality.[30] In other words, even within purely natural considerations, Pomponazzi expresses his basic concern for eternity by admitting a kind of residual immortality, one that does not depend on an infinite extension in time, but is fully realized in the actual experience of the present moment.

Thus the Renaissance left more than one heritage to later thought, on immortality as well as on many other issues. Ficino's concept of immortality as a postulate foreshadows Kant's treatment of the problem in his moral philosohy, although Kant would agree with Pomponazzi that the traditional proofs cannot be accepted as theoretically valid. On the other hand, Pomponazzi's residual immortality as a participation of the present in the eternal anticipates Spinoza and, perhaps, Hegel.

In recent thought the problem of immortality has been much neglected under the impact of positivism. Philosophers have

29. *Ibid.,* ch. 1.
30. *Ibid.,* ch. 7.

tended to treat it as a theological problem that is of no concern to
them, completely forgetting the philosophical origin of the theory.
No attempt to revive the doctrine of immortality on the basis of
linguistic analysis has yet come to my attention, although I should
not be surprised if this were to be done. Theologians, on the other
hand, have been so eager to come to terms with modern science,
that some of them have been quite ready to sacrifice that part of
their heritage that is derived from Greek philosophy, even if that
meant to undo the work of the apologists and Church Fathers to
an extent that goes far beyond the intentions or practice of the
sixteenth-century reformers. I am not sure whether we can revive
the metaphysical doctrine of individual immortality, and I do not
feel committed to such an enterprise. Yet, I strongly believe that
our individual life, every part and every moment of it, belongs to
the universe of nature and of history and is, as such, eternal. Our
life is immortal insofar as in the comprehensive reality of the
universe or, if you wish, of God, everything that once was or will
be is eternally present. I find this view not only necessary as a
comfort in the face of constant change and destruction, but also as
an indispensable counterpart of death. Some residual notion of
immortality seems to correspond to a basic and ineradicable need
and desire of human nature and to be irrefutable by facts or reasons. I should like to think that the teachings of Renaissance and
other thinkers concerning the immortality of the soul, though
expressed in crude and often untenable forms, may be interpreted
as respectable attempts to deal with one of the permanent problems of human life and thought. The problem is still with us, and
we may hope that it may yet lead to new answers that are more in
accordance with our knowledge and our sensibilities than those
transmitted to us by the thinkers of the past, especially those of the
fifteenth and sixteenth centuries.

3. The Unity of Truth

Unlike the dignity of man and the immortality of the soul, the unity of truth has been discussed by recent thinkers no less than by those of the Renaissance or of other periods of the past. Naturally, the terms of this discussion have varied at different times and places. The conflict or harmony between religion and the sciences has been a problem for many thoughtful writers for a long time, and the most thoughtful of them have tried to reconcile their religious beliefs not only with the findings of the natural sciences, but also with historical scholarship, with philosophical reasoning, and with all of secular learning. The increasing acquaintance of Western scholars with other cultures, and especially with the old civilizations of Asia, has led to a demand for reconciling the traditions and the thought of East and West. In the last few years we have heard a good deal about the two cultures, the sciences and the humanities, and the need for harmonizing them, and it would not be difficult to show that there are, in fact, more than two cultures that make a claim on our time and attention, on our curiosity and intellectual allegiance. The unity of science has been proclaimed as an immediate goal by a group of influential philosophers, and in the current chaos of philosophical opinion where different schools seem to ignore rather than to refute each other, at least one lonely voice has advocated their reunion.[1] Our time, no less and perhaps even more than other times, has been puzzled by the actual diversity and competing claims of different philosophical positions, cultural orientations, and intellectual or professional traditions. The desire to attain a kind of harmony or synthesis seems natural enough, and the attempts to satisfy this desire are numerous, but they vary in scope and persuasiveness; and in their very effort to achieve a unity, they often produce new divisions. These attempts have always taken a number of typical forms. One way out of the confusion is always to assert one's own position in a dogmatic fashion and to impose it on others by propaganda or force, if not by strength of argument, while rejecting all other alternatives as false or irrelevant. Another attempt is the position known as skepticism in ancient, and as relativism in modern times. This position treats all philosophical and other opinions as erroneous, and leads us to a state of resignation in which we quietly accept the fact that we cannot know anything for certain and that all the claims made upon our intellectual assent are basically unfounded. This relativism may be given a slightly positive turn, and it becomes a kind of perspectivism that admits all different views, not as simply false, but as partly true. And Hegel made the ambitious attempt to construct a system in which each position, however conflicting with others, is assigned its place as a particular moment of truth. If we look at the confusing multiplicity of opinions and insights, of cultures and traditions, we are impelled to admit that the desire to transform this multiplicity into unity, the conflict into harmony or synthesis, is as natural and inevitable as it is difficult or impossible to achieve. The unity of truth is in my view a regulative idea in the Kantian sense. It imposes on us the task of bringing together into a single system the scattered and

1. Morton White, *Toward Reunion in Philosophy* (Cambridge, Mass., 1956).

apparently irreconcilable insights we derive from different sources, but this task is never ending not only because the elements of knowledge now given to us cannot be reconciled, but because the quest and discovery of new insights will always continue as long as there will be human beings.

The problem of the unity of truth had a comparable, though not identical, significance for the Renaissance as it has had for modern times. In the history of philosophical thought, of science and learning, the Renaissance was an age of fermentation rather than of synthesis. It inherited from the Middle Ages the problem of reconciling philosophy, and especially Aristotelian philosophy, with Christian theology. With the revived interest in ancient literature and thought, Renaissance thinkers and scholars again were confronted with the problem that the Church Fathers had faced: how the substance of classical literature and of ancient philosophies other than Aristotelian could be absorbed and amalgamated, although this problem assumed quite different forms and dimensions from those of late antiquity. The thought of the fifteenth and sixteenth centuries is full of varied attempts to restate specific ancient or medieval positions or to arrive at new combinations or original solutions. The variety of new sources and of old and new opinions and positions brought many thinkers face to face with the question of how this diversity of purported truths could be brought to a unity. In facing this task Renaissance thinkers were able to draw on a variety of ancient and medieval precedents, which they tended to adapt to their own problems and ideas. Late ancient thought, confronted with the conflicting claims and results of different schools and traditions, offered to the attentive reader several fully developed forms of skepticism, both the Academic skepticism known from the writings of Cicero and the Pyrrhonian skepticism preserved by Sextus Empiricus.[2] Cicero and other

2. Richard H. Popkin, *The History of Scepticism from Erasmus to Descartes* (Assen, 1960); Charles B. Schmitt, *Gianfrancesco Pico della Mirandola (1469–1533) and His Critique of Aristotle* (The Hague, 1967).

writers presented the example of that eclecticism that had pre-vailed among the Middle Stoics and the Middle Platonists. Finally, the writings of the Neoplatonists and, in a sense, also those of Aristotle provided the model for a philosophical synthesis that tried to comprehend all that was valid in the thought of previous thinkers while rejecting their errors. Medieval thought, on the other hand, provided the Renaissance with a large arsenal of argu-ments, formulated in terms of many different issues, for the discus-sion of the relationship between faith and reason, philosophy and theology, as well as with a few general attempts to define this relationship: the harmony between faith and reason or the con-firmation of faith by reason, as proposed by Aquinas; the gradual withdrawal of reason from the area of faith and the tendency to base theological doctrine on faith and authority alone, which we may notice in the schools of Duns Scotus and William of Ockam; and finally the coexistence of faith and reason that grants to faith a superior validity, but not the right to interfere in the domain of reason, a position known under the crude label "double truth theory" and usually associated with Latin Averroism but actually found in the work of many thinkers who cannot be considered followers of Averroes in any precisely definable sense. We shall try to describe as best we can how some of the Renaissance thinkers dealt with the same insistent and elusive problem, and what use, if any, they made of the various solutions placed at their disposal by their ancient and medieval predecessors.

In discussing the views of some Renaissance thinkers on this subject, I shall begin this time with Pomponazzi, the representa-tive of the Aristotelian school, since his attitude is most closely connected with the medieval tradition, at least on this particular issue. In his famous treatise on the Immortality of the Soul, Pomponazzi carefully distinguishes, both at the beginning and at the end, between that which is true and most certain in itself and must be accepted as such on the basis of faith and that which can be proven within natural limits and in accordance with the teachings of Aristotle.[3] The immortality of the soul must be accepted as an article of faith, as we saw in the preceding essay, but it cannot be demonstrated on natural or Aristotelian grounds. In other words, although Pomponazzi rejects in his treatise the specific position of Averroes according to which there is only one intellect both active and passive for all men, he adopts on the relation of faith and reason, theology and philosophy a view, that has been crudely labeled the double truth theory, and that had been associated during the preceding centuries, primarily if not exclusively, with the tradition of Latin Averroism. This doctrine, which we might more fairly describe as a separation or dualism of faith and reason, has been much discussed by modern historians and has received from them a varied interpretation. Since the position evidently considers the teachings of faith and of reason incompatible in a plain and simple sense and since thinkers such as Pomponazzi display a great deal of acumen and persistence in setting forth the arguments of reason, many scholars have inferred that Pomponazzi, and other thinkers using the same line of reasoning, were not sincere, but merely adopted the dualistic theory as a protective device to cover their real but secret disbelief against ecclesiastic censure. Among the historians who have adopted this view, those who themselves held strong convictions of a secular and anticlerical, if not outright atheistic nature, praised Pomponazzi and the Averroists as the standard-bearers of modern free thought in a period otherwise oppressed by religious conformism; whereas some others, who favored the medieval Catholic view of the world, concurred in the assumption that the double truth theory was hypocritical but reversed the value judgment and condemned the hypocrisy, as well as the underlying disbelief, in no uncertain terms.[4] Leaving aside the question whether and to what

3. Prologue and ch. 15.
4. P. O. Kristeller, "The Myth of Renaissance Atheism and the French Tradition of Free Thought," *Journal of the History of Philosophy,* 6 (1968): 233–243.

extent it is the business of the historian, and especially of the historian of philosophy, to heap praise or blame on the victims of his interpretation, I am inclined to doubt the basic assumption that Pomponazzi wrote his statements on faith and reason in bad faith. I find no textual evidence for such a view, and I do not purport to possess special devices, chemical or intuitive, that bring forth the secret thoughts which an author wrote with invisible ink between his lines or kept in his mind without committing them to writing. I rather leave the burden of proof to those who make such claims, and stand for the time being on the written record as I think the historian, not unlike the judge, is obliged to do. If we make the contrary assumption, namely that an author meant to say what he said, an assumption which is not always wrong, we will come out with the conclusion that Pomponazzi, one of the most honest and acute thinkers of the Renaissance, found himself in a genuine dilemma when he was forced to admit, as in the case of immortality, that there was a discrepancy between the conclusions of reason and Aristotle and the teachings of the Church. I am inclined to admit that the dualistic theory, unsatisfactory as it may seem to us, is one of the possible attempts to deal with a genuine dilemma, and specifically with a case where there is an insoluble discrepancy between philosophy and theology, between reason and faith. I should even say that for a thinker who wanted to hold on to both reason and faith and found himself confronted with such a discrepancy, this is the most plausible manner in which he can face, if not solve, the dilemma. For somebody who is willing to do either without reason or without faith or without both, the dilemma ceases to exist, and the theory loses its purpose and meaning. But we have no basis to assume that this was the case of Pomponazzi or of his predecessors or contemporaries who adopted the same or a similar position.

It is interesting to note that the different interpretations of Pomponazzi's view which we have encountered in modern historians were expressed already in his own time and shortly afterwards by his friends and opponents, but this is a subject which we cannot pursue in this essay. Instead, I should like to emphasize the contribution made by Pomponazzi's dualism to the discussion of the problem with which we are concerned. Faced with the competing claims of religion and philosophy and committed to uphold both of them, Pomponazzi in substance defends the view that faith and reason are each master in its own domain, and thus he opens the way for a genuine dualism or even pluralism that makes allowance for different sources of truth. I am convinced that his position still deserves examination on the part of theologians conscious of the competing claims of the sciences and of secular learning and on the part of scientists and philosophers tolerant of the claims that religion or art or other areas of human experience may make upon our thought. Perhaps this might be a way for us to deal with the "two cultures," or rather with the many cultures that are contained in the complex texture of our life and knowledge.

If we pass from the Aristotelians to the typical humanist scholars of the Renaissance, our problem appears in less precise outlines, as might have been expected, but still is felt to be present in several distinct ways. One type of discussion that seems to be relevant to our topic is the widespread debate about the relative superiority of the various arts and sciences. There is a whole literature on the merits of medicine and law that has received some recent attention.[5] There is a similar discussion on arms and letters,[6] and the superior claims of different arts and sciences found

5. Coluccio Salutati, *De nobilitate legum et medicinae,* ed. E. Garin (Florence, 1947); *La disputa della arti nel Quattrocento,* ed. E. Garin (Florence, 1947); G. F. Pagallo, "Nuovi testi per la 'Disputa delle arti' nel Quattrocento . . . ," *Italia Medioevale e Umanistica,* 2 (1959): 467–481; Kristeller, *Renaissance Thought* (1961), p. 157. A "sermo habitus in initio studii sub questione de praestantia medicinae et scientiae legalis" by Julianus Bononiensis dates from the early fourteenth century (ms. Vat. lat. 2418, cf. Kristeller, *Iter Italicum,* Vol. 2 [Leyden, 1967]: p. 313).

6. It flourished in the sixteenth century. Yet the fifteenth-century humanist Lapo da Castiglionchio wrote a *comparatio inter rem militarem et studia literarum* that occurs in several manuscripts (e.g., Florence, ms. Ricc. 149, f. 64–84, cf. *Iter Italicum,* Vol. 1 [Leyden, 1963]: p. 187).

eloquent defenders, frequently, and by pure coincidence, among
their own professional representatives. A famous example is Leonardo's *Paragone,* in which the superiority of painting over other
arts and sciences is argued in some detail.[7] This kind of literature
is merely a part of a broader humanist tendency to indulge in the
praise or blame of different pursuits and in the comparison of
those thought to be in competition with each other. It is a manner
of reasoning that is also found in some areas of medieval literature
but which goes back, as a general pattern, to ancient rhetorical
theory and literature which became much better known during the
Renaissance. Especially important for the humanists was, of
course, the defense of their own studies against the claims of other
disciplines, most frequently against theology but occasionally also
against medicine or other fields. This literature is best known
under the label "the defense of poetry," and we find it in the work
of Petrarch and before him in Mussato and again in Boccaccio and
Salutati and in some writers of the later fifteenth century.[8] The
label should not deceive us, for by "poetry" these authors do not
understand, as a modern reader might suspect, the composition of
vernacular verse, but rather the composition of Latin poetry, and
above all, the study and interpretation of the ancient poets and of
other classical writers and even the entire cycle of learning, the
studia humanitatis, with which the humanists were concerned and

7. Leonardo da Vinci, *Paragone, A Comparison of the Arts,* ed. I. A.
Richter (London, 1949).
8. For Mussato's poetic reply to Frater Johanninus de Mantua O.P., see
Thesaurus Antiquitatum et Historiarum Italiae, ed. Jo. Georg. Graevius,
Vol. 6, pt. 2 (Leyden, 1722), cols. 59–62. Petrarch, *De sui ipsius et multorum
ignorantia,* ed. L. M. Capelli (Paris, 1906); *Invective contra medicum,* ed.
P. G. Ricci (Rome, 1950); G. Boccaccio, *Genealogie deorum gentilium
libri,* ed. V. Romano, 2 vols. (Bari, 1951), books XIV and XV (Vol. 2,
pp. 679–785). Colucii Salutati *De laboribus Herculis,* ed. B. L. Ullman,
2 vols. (Zurich, 1951). Around the middle of the fifteenth century, a
Regular Canon, Timoteo Maffei, wrote a similar treatise addressed to
Nicolaus V and entitled *In sanctam rusticitatem* that appears in a number
of manuscripts (e.g., Florence, Laurenziana, ms. Ashb. 690, fasc. 2; cf. *Iter
Italicum,* 1: 89–90).

from which they derived their own name. In defending the study of the classical poets against their theological critics, the humanists used some of the arguments advanced by the Church Fathers and often insisted that the pagan poems and the myths contained in them had an allegorical meaning that was compatible and in fundamental agreement with the truth of Christian religion. The faith in allegory and in the harmony or parallelism of ancient and Christian wisdom had a very great importance in the thought, literature, and art of the Renaissance and of the subsequent period down to the eighteenth century.[9] Allegory has gone out of fashion since, and its somewhat crude application to the defense of ancient literature is no longer to our taste. But the claim that poetry and the other arts reveal their own truths, compatible with those of religion and of the sciences, or even superior to them, has found many defenders among romantic and later literary critics, as well as in modern philosophical thought.

In another sense, the humanists had to face the problem of truth in their discussion of straight philosophical and especially of moral problems which they considered to be a part of their legitimate domain. Uninterested as most of them were in a precise method or terminology, in a systematic presentation of their thought, or even in the content of cosmology or metaphysics, they were encouraged by the example of Cicero, their favorite ancient author, to borrow individual ideas or sentences from a great variety of ancient authors and to adapt them rather freely and flexibly to their own thought and writing. Ciceronianism in thought, as distinct from mere style or rhetorical doctrine, is the equivalent of eclecticism, and the moral writings of the humanists, from Petrarch to Montaigne, are full of quotations or adapted ideas taken from the most diverse ancient writers—technical philosophers as well as moralists, orators, poets, or historians. Not the authors whom modern scholarship considers as the greatest

9. E. Wind, *Pagan Mysteries in the Renaissance* (New Haven, 1958).

thinkers of antiquity were favored, but rather Cicero and Seneca
among the Latins, Isocrates, Plutarch, and Lucian among the
Greeks, authors whom modern scholarship studies for the information they contain on earlier and more original thinkers rather than
for their own sake but who appealed to the humanists through
their terse sentences and striking anecdotes. Ancient quotations
were treated as authorities, that is, as a special kind of rhetorical
argument, and each humanist kept his own commonplace book as
fruit of his readings for later writing, doubly important at a time
when there were no dictionaries or indices to speak of. Finally,
Erasmus with his *Adagia* earned the gratitude of posterity by sup-
plying his successors with a systematic collection of anecdotes and
sentences ready for use, the real quotation book of the early
modern period that everybody used but few cared to mention.
Superficial as humanist eclecticism tended to be, much more
superficial than its ancient counterpart, it still had the merit of
broadening the sources of thought and information that an individual moralist was ready to use. It reflects the wide curiosity of
the age, more eager to draw freely upon a vast range of undigested
ideas than to submit a narrow body of authoritative texts to minute
logical analysis, as the preceding period had tended to do.

Aside from the eclectic use of ancient ideas, especially in the
area of moral thought, the chief impact of classical humanism on
Renaissance philosophy was the revival of ancient philosophical
doctrines other than Aristotelianism. Of special relevance to our
problem is the revival of ancient skepticism that we may observe in
several thinkers and writers of the fifteenth, and especially of the
sixteenth century.[10] The skeptical position insists that all philosophical doctrines may be refuted and is, on the face of it, quite
negative with reference to the attainment of truth. But ever since
antiquity, skepticism has proclaimed itself to be bringing about
intellectual freedom, since it liberates its adherents from the

10. See note 2 above.

narrow restraints of fixed doctrines.[11] Moreover, the skeptical doctrine enabled its followers to approve any number of specific thoughts in an eclectic fashion, provided they admitted that these thoughts were merely probable and not strictly certain or demonstrable. Occasionally, a skeptic such as Montaigne would even grant that there is a single and immutable truth but add that this truth cannot be grasped by any human being, at least not in its entirety.[12] In the Renaissance skepticism often entered an alliance with a kind of fideism, as in the thought of Gianfrancesco Pico or in Montaigne, in a manner that had a precedent in Augustine but was, of course, quite unknown to the Greek skeptics.[13] That is, whereas it is possible to refute and thus to discard any definite statement in the field of philosophy and of secular learning, religious doctrine, based on faith and authority alone, would be exempt from this rule of uncertainty and thus provide us with a firm belief that cannot be shaken by any rational arguments.

Another ancient philosophical school that was revived in the wake of humanism was Platonism, and it was Renaissance Platonism that, in my opinion, made the most interesting contributions to our problem. Here we find the tendency not only to establish a harmony between religion and philosophy, thus overcoming the dualism of the Aristotelians and the Skeptics, and in a sense returning on a different level to the Thomist position, but also to recognize that there is a comprehensive universal truth in which the doctrines of each school or individual thinker merely participated, thus reasserting in a more positive fashion the intellectual variety and liberty at which the eclectics and skeptics had aimed.

The general view is clearly implied in the thought of Nicolaus Cusanus. In his metaphysics each particular being is nothing but a

11. Eugene F. Rice, *The Renaissance Idea of Wisdom* (Cambridge, Mass., 1958), pp. 187–190.

12. Montaigne, *Essais*, ed. J. Plattard, Vol. 2, pt. 1 (Paris, 1947), p. 326.

13. For Gianfrancesco Pico, see Schmitt (note 2 above). For Montaigne, see Donald M. Frame, *Montaigne's Discovery of Man* (New York, 1955), pp. 57–73.

particular manifestation or contraction of the one infinite and divine principle, and, in the same way, each human doctrine is but a special expression of the universal truth that can never be expressed in any one particular statement. On this basis, it is possible for Cusanus to find a partial truth in a variety of philosophical and religious doctrines, including Mohammedanism.[14]

What in Cusanus is a pervasive conception closely linked with the center of his metaphysics, appears in the Florentine Academy and its followers as a series of articulate, though not always fully developed statements. In the work of its leader, Marsilio Ficino, we find several concepts pointing toward the idea of a universal truth. First of all, he insists on a basic harmony between Platonic philosophy and Christian theology. In trying to defend the immortality of the soul, which he considered essential for religion and theology, and to refute the Averroist doctrine of the unity of the intellect, which he considered incompatible with immortality, he insisted that his opponents had destroyed the harmony between religion and philosophy and that he himself had been destined by providence to restore that unity.[15] Yet, in his attempt to establish the harmony between philosophy and theology, he goes a long way toward putting them on the same level, calling religion and philosophy sisters and claiming that they are different expressions of the same basic truth.[16] In thus raising philosophy to the level of theology (and he called his chief philosophical work *Platonic Theology*), Ficino goes not only beyond his Thomist predecessors, but also beyond his Aristotelian opponents. Moreover, although Ficino often speaks exclusively in terms of Platonic philosophy and Christian theology, his horizon of truth is somewhat larger than we might expect. Not only does he consider ancient Judaism as the true predecessor of Christian doctrine, as orthodoxy required, but

14. E. Cassirer, *The Individual and the Cosmos in Renaissance Philosophy,* trans. M. Domandi (New York, 1963), pp. 28–31.

15. Kristeller, *The Philosophy of Marsilio Ficino* (New York, 1943), pp. 27–29.

16. *Ibid.,* pp. 320–323.

he also asserts that all other religions are based on man's fundamental desire for God, that they all aim, though unconsciously, at
the one true God, and that they are all species of the same genus
religion of which Christianity constitutes the most perfect species.[17]
A similar tendency toward a broader tolerance may be noticed in
Ficino's view of the history of philosophy. Following the precedent
of his Neoplatonic and Byzantine predecessors, Ficino considers
the works attributed to Hermes Trismegistus, Zoroaster, Orpheus,
and Pythagoras, which modern scholarship has recognized as
forgeries of late antiquity, to be genuine monuments of ancient
pagan wisdom, Oriental and Greek. Ficino insists on the doctrinal
affinity between these writings and those of Plato and his school
and treats the ancient sages, reputed authors of these writings, as
predecessors and teachers of Plato. In his view, they form an
ancient tradition of pagan theology and philosophy that is as old as
that of the Hebrew and Christian religion, going back to Mercurius
Trismegistus, a contemporary of Moses. Thus there arises in his
view a more or less continuous tradition in two different but parallel branches, philosophical or pagan and religious or Hebrew and
Christian that extends in a nearly continuous line from the early
days of Moses and Trismegistus down to his own day.[18] In the
history of philosophy proper, there are a good many schools and
doctrines whom he rejects, but he is obviously eager to absorb as
many authors as possible into his synthesis, as we may see from
the variety of writers whom he quotes as authorities for specific
ideas he endorses. Apart from the Platonic tradition, Ficino respects and utilizes Aristotle and his commentators, and even Epicurus and Lucretius, much more frequently and openly than we
might expect, and it is apparent that his Platonism, rightly so
called since he admires Plato and his school above all, tends to be
inclusive rather than exclusive as far as other schools and thinkers
are concerned.

17. *Ibid.*, pp. 316–320.
18. *Ibid.*, pp. 25–27.

Ficino's younger friend and associate, Giovanni Pico della Mirandola, went much further than his teacher in his conception of
universal truth, and he gave the doctrine of universal truth a
classical formulation that is most representative of the Renaissance period and has remained most famous ever since. In emphasizing the similar elements in the work of Ficino, I did not intend
to diminish Pico's merit, but rather tried to show how and to what
extent Ficino had prepared the ground for Pico's much more
developed ideas on the subject.

For Pico, the idea that truth is universal and that thinkers of all
philosophical and religious traditions have a part in it is one of his
most pervasive and fundamental assumptions. And it is closely
connected with his idea of liberty, for he keeps telling us that we
should not be limited to the teachings of a single thinker or school
but should study all thinkers of the past to discover the truth
contained in their writings. It is this conviction that a share of
truth may be found in the works of thinkers of all times, places,
and religions that motivates and justifies the vast scholarly curiosity for which Pico has rightly become famous. This universal
curiosity is reflected in Pico's training and in his library. He had a
humanist education that comprised a solid knowledge of classical
Greek and Latin literature, and he had also a scholastic training
acquired both at Padua and Paris that gave him an unusual familiarity with the philosophical and theological writers of the Middle
Ages. This combination of humanistic and scholastic training was
unusual, at least in its extent, and it explains why Pico, though
recognized as a consummate humanist by his friends and contemporaries, went out of his way to defend the scholastics against
Ermolao Barbaro. Through his contact with Ficino, he acquired a
thorough familiarity with the authentic and apocryphal sources of
Platonism. But his curiosity went further. Pico learned Hebrew,
Aramaic, and Arabic, and he had the works of many Arabic and
Hebrew writers that had been unknown to Western scholars explained or translated for his use. This applies to Averroes and

other Arabic thinkers, to the Jewish commentators on the Old Testament, and to the Jewish Cabalists. Pico's conviction that the Cabalists were in basic agreement with Christian theology gave rise to a whole current of Christian Cabalism that remained alive for several centuries and has attracted much scholarly attention in recent years. And the vast variety of sources used by Pico appears not only in his library, but also in his writings.[19]

The most direct expression of Pico's belief that truth may be discovered in the writings of many authors and schools is found in the 900 theses, which Pico put together in 1486 for a public disputation he intended to hold in Rome during the following year and which was subsequently prohibited by Pope Innocent VIII, after a papal commission had examined the theses and found some of them to be heretical or dubious. The theses cover philosophy, theology, and several other fields, and some of them are presented as expressing Pico's own opinion. Yet a large number are explicitly taken from the writings of a great variety of thinkers. Among the authors used we find not only Albert, Thomas, and Duns Scotus, but also several other medieval scholastics, then Averroes, Avicenna, and several other Arabic and Jewish thinkers, then a number of Greek Aristotelian and Neoplatonic philosophers, the ancient theologians such as Pythagoras and Trismegistus, and finally the Cabalists.[20] The combination of so many authors whose views had given rise to competing schools clearly implies Pico's conviction that their teachings, or at least some of them, may be reconciled in a comprehensive doctrine, and this tendency becomes curiously evident in another thesis where Pico claims that the unity of the intellect may be reconciled with the immortality of

19. Kristeller, "Giovanni Pico della Mirandola and His Sources," in *L'Opera e il Pensiero di Giovanni Pico della Mirandola,* I (Florence, 1965): 35–133. Cf. P. Kibre, *The Library of Pico della Mirandola* (New York, 1936). For his Cabalism, see J. Blau, *The Christian Interpretation of the Cabala in the Renaissance* (New York, 1944); F. Secret, *Les kabbalistes chrétiens de la Renaissance* (Paris, 1964).

20. Jo. Picus, *Opera* (Basel, 1572), pp. 63–113.

the soul, a view to which neither Ficino nor Pomponazzi would have subscribed.[21]

Yet, the notion that all thinkers have a share in truth is not merely implied by the choice of authors cited in the theses, but it is explicitly set forth in the Oration Pico composed for the disputation. This Oration, which has been preserved for us in an early draft (discovered by Garin) and in a posthumous edition, as eloquently treats in its second part the universality of truth as its first part deals with the dignity of man. It also is apparent that the universality of truth constitutes the theme which is meant to announce and justify the disputation of the theses, and hence this section was repeated with but minor changes in the *Apologia*, which Pico published in 1487 after the condemnation of some of his theses. "Pledged to the doctrines of no man," Pico says, "I have ranged through all the masters of philosophy, investigated all books, and come to know all schools." He adds that each school, and each philosopher, has some distinctive merit, and he praises in turn the philosophers whose doctrines he is going to defend. "This has been my reason for wishing to bring before the public the opinions not of a single school alone . . . but rather of every school to the end that the light of truth. . . . through this comparison of several sects and this discussion of manifold philosophies might dawn more brightly on our minds."[22] But not content with repeating the truths discovered by others, Pico claims to add some of his own and proceeds to justify some of his own teachings set forth in the remainder of the theses. Still more concisely, the underlying idea appears in the early version of the speech: "There has been nobody in the past, and there will be nobody after us, to whom truth has given itself to be understood in its entirety. Its immensity is too great for human capacity to be equal to it."[23]

21. See Chapter 2, note 23.
22. *De hominis dignitate,* ed. Garin (1942), pp. 138–142.
23. Garin, *La cultura filosofica del Rinascimento italiano* (Florence, 1961), p. 239.

Pico's notion of truth shares with the skeptics the rejection of the dogmatic claims of any particular master or school and with the eclectics the intellectual freedom to choose from the writings of any philosopher what seems to be true or useful. Yet, unlike the eclectics, he does not choose at random what he pleases, but he seems to be guided by an intuitive certainty of what is true (and this he derives from the Platonist tradition); and unlike the skeptics he does not stress the inadequacy that separates all human opinion from the absolute truth, but rather the positive share it derives from that truth. Pico does not believe with Hegel that every philosophical position as a whole constitutes, as it were, a form of truth. He rather thinks (and this idea he derives from the scholastic tradition) that the work of every thinker is made up of a great number of specific statements and that the truth or falsity of any one of them does not stand or fall with that of all others. He feels perfectly free to reject the views of any past thinker on any particular point, but he is convinced that the work of every philosopher worthy of the name contains some true statements and that the presence of these true statements makes the philosopher worth studying and justifies the effort we may have to make to study his language and to read his writings. At the same time, Pico does not think that the study of past opinions leaves us no room for new or original thoughts. In combining or recombining the views expressed by our predecessors, we already give them a form and synthesis that differs from any one of them, and in adopting or criticizing their opinions, we clear the ground for advancing new and more valid opinions of our own. Thus, Pico voices a supreme confidence in the value of both learning and originality, and the only reservation we may have to make about it is that while what he offers us is, to be sure, a magnificent program, he was prevented, and perhaps not only through his early death, from working it out in a concrete and viable system. Yet, if we take his view of universal truth not as an established doctrine, but as a regulative idea, it is still as suggestive as it was in Pico's own time.

Only the specific ideas and traditions and elements of knowledge that are given to us and that we must try to harmonize are different from those of the Renaissance.

Before we leave our subject, we must briefly discuss another Renaissance author who belonged to the school of Ficino and Pico and who was much less famous or distinguished than either of them. This author is Augustino Steuco, a liberal Catholic theologian of the mid-sixteenth century. Restating and developing with great learning the views of the Renaissance Platonists, he chose for his main work a title that summed up their aspirations in a new way and that was to have a persistent appeal through the subsequent centuries up to the present: the perennial philosophy.[24] The notion of a perennial philosophy, of a wisdom that pervades the entire history of human thought, although it may be obscured in each instance by false or irrelevant ideas, has been expressed a number of times even in our century; although, in effect, many different systems of thought have claimed, each for itself, to represent this perennial philosophy. Most frequently the term has been used in connection with Thomism, and hence some scholars, who knew the title but not the content of Steuco's work, have thought that he was a Thomist. Actually, Steuco was a Renaissance Platonist, and the perennial philosophy which he had in mind was the doctrine of Platonism, represented by Plato and his ancient and early modern followers but also by his supposed early predecessors. Steuco, in effect, conceived a Plato who was in basic agreement with Aristotle and other ancient philosophers on a number of points and, above all, with Jewish and Christian theology. The label "perennial philosophy" turned out to be fortunate, and the term was taken up by many later thinkers, whether or not they shared Steuco's philosophical position or even were aware of it. It is a term that may be used for the claims of a special school, but in its original intent it reflects the idea, best expressed by Pico,

24. Charles B. Schmitt, "Perennial Philosophy: From Agostino Steuco to Leibniz," *Journal of the History of Ideas,* 27 (1966): 505–532.

of a universal truth that is beyond any particular human doctrine but in which each doctrine, if worthy of that name, has a share. The idea of the perennial philosophy imposes upon us the task of keeping it alive by trying to grasp and synthesize every element of truth given to us by the earlier thinkers and traditions which are accessible to us and by adding to it whatever we may be able to discover for ourselves by the resources of our thought or experience.

We have reached the conclusion of our rapid and somewhat superficial discussion of three major themes of Renaissance thought: the dignity of man, the immortality of the soul, and the unity of truth. We have not tried to exhaust the numerous philosophical and theological doctrines that may be said to add up to such a thing as the Renaissance conception of man. We have merely touched on three aspects of that conception. The praise of man's dignity reflects some of the aspirations of the period and leads to an attempt to assign to man a privileged place in the scheme of things. The doctrine of immortality is, in a way, an extension of man's dignity and individuality beyond the limits of his present life, and, thus, the emphasis on immortality provides, in turn, a horizon for this life itself. The problem of truth may be conceived and treated in different terms, but the angle of it which we have stressed, the quest for the unity of truth in the face of divergent and apparently incompatible doctrines, is again related to man and his concerns. In a moment such as ours when there is so much talk about commitment, it might not be amiss to point out that one of the basic human commitments, and for a philosopher or theologian, scientist or scholar the only legitimate commitment, is the commitment to truth and that there is even some existentialist authority for this statement. But I gladly admit that the problems discussed here represent but a small and arbitrary selection among the philosophical ideas expressed by Renaissance thinkers on man or on any other subject. I have selected them merely because they have impressed me as interesting and charac-

teristic among the ideas found in the work of some Renaissance
authors whom I have read most frequently and most attentively,
although even in the case of these authors, my knowledge and my
understanding obviously have their limitations.

I do not wish to suggest that Renaissance thought, on the
matters we have discussed or on any others, supplies us with ready-
made solutions that we could accept as valid answers to our own
problems. Every period, every generation, every thinking person
must find its own answers, and if we study the history of philosophy or of civilization in search of such ready answers, we are
bound to be disappointed. Past thought is intrinsically interesting,
I believe, because it shows us precedents and analogies for our
problems, and it may enlarge our perspective by putting before us
alternatives of which we had not thought. We should neither un-
critically admire nor imitate the past, or can we afford to completely ignore it. We must know it first before we can take from it
what we can use and approve, while rejecting the rest. I often hear
responsible, or rather irresponsible, educators say that the knowledge of the past, or even our present knowledge, should be adapted
to the needs and interests of our time, and especially of our
younger generation. We should rather stand by our conviction that
some, if not all, of this knowledge is intrinsically true and valid
and that the younger generation will have to absorb it before it can
make any significant contribution of its own. In the long run, it is
not the past that is measured by us, but we ourselves will be
measured by it and judged by it since we have to prove to the
future whether we have lived up to the standards of the past. As it
has been said that nobody can command who has not first learned
to obey, so I should like to say that nobody can create or build
who has not first learned what there is to be learned. Human
civilization is a cumulative process, and any part of it is more
easily and more quickly destroyed than rebuilt. No single generation can hope to build or rebuild it from the bottom, and hence we
should gratefully accept and appreciate the building materials

which past periods no less creative than ours have left to us. It is an inheritance each generation is called upon to hand on to its successor. It cannot help neglecting and destroying a part of this heritage, but it should always try to preserve what is worth preserving and to add something that is better in the place of what has been destroyed.

II The Renaissance and Byzantine Learning

4. *Italian Humanism and Byzantium*

The subject of this paper is vast and complex, and I have neither the time nor the knowledge to treat it as fully as it deserves or even to mention all its facets. I must limit myself to a survey of the facts that are more or less generally accepted and shall merely indicate some of the problems that, in my opinion, should be further investigated.

The Italian humanistic movement of the Renaissance has been the subject of many recent studies and discussions, but there seems to be by now a fairly general agreement that it was a broad and pervasive cultural movement that affected at the same time the literature and philosophy, the historiography and philological scholarship of the period and that also had wide repercussions in theology, in the sciences, and in the arts. In their efforts to determine the sources and the originality of Italian and European humanism, historians have mainly compared it with the Latin Middle Ages and have tried to define the affinities and differences between humanistic culture and the Western culture of the preceding age. The question of Byzantine contacts and influences imposes itself for obvious reasons only in one area of humanistic culture, that is, in the field of Greek studies. It will thus be necessary for us to limit our attention in this paper almost entirely to this area, whereas the contacts between Byzantium and the Italian Renaissance in the field of philosophy will be the subject of another paper.

A discussion of our subject would seem to be most timely since Byzantine studies have been much cultivated during the last few decades. Yet, these studies deal with a period that lasted more than a thousand years, and they have concentrated for the most part on political and economic history, on religious institutions and theological doctrines, on literature, music, and the visual arts but have dealt only to a small extent with classical scholarship and with philosophy. Hence, many questions that from our point of view would be especially important remain to my knowledge still unresolved and are in need of further research.[1]

If we want to understand the state and development of Greek studies in the West during the Middle Ages and the Renaissance, we must go back to classical antiquity, that is, to the Greek culture

1. For the general bibliography of our subject, I should like to cite the following works: N. H. Baynes, *Byzantine Studies and Other Essays* (London, 1955); *Byzantium,* ed. N. H. Baynes and H. St. L. B. Moss (Oxford, 1949); H. G. Beck, *Kirche und theologische Literatur im byzantinischen Reich* (Munich, 1959); R. R. Bolgar, *The Classical Heritage and Its Beneficiaries* (Cambridge, 1954); R. Devreesse, *Introduction à l'étude des manuscrits grecs* (Paris, 1954); Devreesse, *Les manuscrits de l'Italie méridionale* (Vatican City, 1955); A. Ehrhard, *Ueberlieferung und Bestand der hagiographischen und homiletischen Literatur der griechischen Kirche von den Anfaengen bis zum Ende des 16. Jahrhunderts,* 2 vols. (Leipzig, 1937–1952); K. Krumbacher, *Geschichte der byzantinischen Literatur,* 2d ed. (Munich, 1897); E. Legrand, *Bibliographie Hellénique,* 4 vols. (Paris, 1885–1906); K. Oehler, *Antike Philosophie und Byzantinisches Mittelalter* (Munich, 1969); R. Sabbadini, *Le scoperte dei codici latini e greci ne' secoli XIV e XV,* 2 vols. (Florence, 1905–1914); J. E. Sandys, *A History of Classical Scholarship,* Vol. I, 3d ed. (Cambridge, 1921); I. Ševčenko, "The Decline of Byzantium Seen through the Eyes of Its Intellectuals," *Dumbarton Oaks Papers,* 15 (1961): 167–186; B. Tatakis, *La philosophie byzantine* (Paris, 1949); M. Vogel and V. Gardthausen, *Die griechischen Schreiber des Mittelalters und der Renaissance* (Leipzig, 1909); G. Voigt, *Die Wiederbelebung des classischen Alterthums,* 3d ed., 2 vols. (Berlin, 1893).

of the Romans; for the foundation of medieval Western culture
was Latin and not Greek. During the later Republic and the first
centuries of the Empire most educated Romans knew Greek, and
many of them even wrote in Greek, as did Marcus Aurelius. At the
same time Latin literature developed under the continuing influence of Greek models, and the small number of Latin writings that
dealt with philosophical or scientific subjects is entirely derived
from Greek sources.[2] Also Latin Christianity derived its scriptures
and its theology from the Greek East. With the end of antiquity
and the beginning of the Middle Ages, the Latin West not only
became separated from the Greco-Byzantine East in a political
sense, but it also lost the knowledge of the Greek language and
thus its direct access to ancient Greek culture.[3] Hence, the first
medieval centuries, up to the middle of the eleventh century, were
largely restricted to the literary, philosophical, and scientific resources of the Latin tradition. This tradition was rich in concepts
and ideas, literary forms, and rhetorical and poetical theory and
practice of Greek origin, but it possessed or, at least, preserved but
very few translations of Greek texts. The Latins had above all the
Bible and many writings of the Greek Fathers, a part of Plato's
Timaeus, the *Categories* and *De interpretatione* of Aristotle with
Porphyry's *Introduction to the Categories,* in the translation of
Boethius, and some medical and mathematical writings. That large
and important part of classical Greek literature which had not
been translated into Latin was not accessible to the first centuries
of the Latin Middle Ages, and the significance of this fact seems to
have escaped some recent historians of that important period.

This situation changed to some extent, but only to some extent,
during the period that extends from the second half of the eleventh
century to the end of the thirteenth or the first half of the fourteenth. Historians of that period have rightly emphasized the

2. W. Stahl, *Roman Science* (Madison, Wis., 1962).
3. P. Courcelle, *Les lettres grecques en Occident, De Macrobe à
Cassiodore* (Paris, 1943).

continued or resumed contacts of the West with Byzantium in the political and economic fields, in church affairs, and in the arts, and they have also stressed the continued presence of the Greek language and culture in Sicily and in some parts of Southern Italy. The Crusades and the Latin conquest of the Byzantine Empire had their repercussions also in the area of intellectual history. This period produced a sizable number of Latin translations of ancient Greek texts that had never been translated at the time of antiquity or of the early Middle Ages. Some of these translations were made from the Arabic, others, directly from the Greek. The Greco-Latin translations evidently presuppose both some knowledge of Greek on the part of the translators and some access to the Greek texts.[4] There were also several attempts, especially at the time of the Council of Vienne, to introduce the teaching of Greek at some of the major universities.

These facts should be duly considered, but we should also note their limited significance and should not exaggerate their importance. We know from other medieval and modern examples that political and commercial contacts and even artistic influences do not require a close acquaintance with the language or civilization of the country of origin. Hence, they do not always lead to scientific or literary influences since the latter depend on such an acquaintance and also presuppose in him who learns a genuine interest in the characteristic values of a foreign civilization. The fact that Greek was spoken in Sicily and Southern Italy does not indicate by itself a flourishing state of Greek classical studies unless there was also some knowledge of the classical Greek language, some Greek

4. C. H. Haskins, *Studies in the History of Mediaeval Science,* 2d ed. (Cambridge, Mass., 1927); J. T. Muckle, "Greek Works Translated Directly into Latin before 1350," *Mediaeval Studies,* 4 (1942): 33–42; 5 (1943): 102–114; G. Sarton, *Introduction to the History of Science,* 3 vols. (Baltimore, Md., 1927–1948); A. Siegmund, *Die Ueberlieferung der griechischen christlichen Literatur in der lateinischen Kirche bis zum zwoelften Jahrhundert* (Munich-Pasing, 1949); M. Steinschneider, *Die europaeischen Uebersetzungen aus dem Arabischen bis Mitte de 17. Jahrhunderts* (Graz, 1957).

classical texts in the libraries of the region, and some tradition of classical and not only ecclesiastic studies in the monastic or city schools of the area. We have recently learned a good deal about the libraries and the manuscripts and also about the literary production of Greek Italy but so far very little about its schools and studies.[5] At the present state of our knowledge I am not convinced that Greek classical studies in the West were as strongly influenced by Greek Italy as they were by Greece herself, and especially by Constantinople. Greek Italy made, no doubt, its contribution to Byzantine civilization, and not only in the field of theology; but in the case of some of its notable representatives, such as Johannes Italos or Barlaam of Calabria, it is probable that they received their classical education, at least in part, at Constantinople rather than at home. To my knowledge, there is not yet any evidence that Greek Italy had her own indigenous tradition in the field of classical studies, as was the case in ecclesiastic learning or in Byzantine literature.

If we pass from Greek Italy to the rest of Latin Europe, the traces of Greek learning are very scanty indeed.[6] The decrees intended to introduce the study of Greek at the universities remained, for the most part, a dead letter, and we have no clear case

5. R. Devreesse, *Les manuscrits grecs de l'Italie méridionale* (Vatican City, 1955); M. Gigante, *Poeti italobizantini del secolo XIII* (Naples, 1953); Barlaam Calabro, *Epistole greche,* ed. G. Schirò (Palermo, 1954); K. Setton, "The Byzantine Background to the Italian Renaissance," *Proceedings of the American Philosophical Society,* 100 (1956): 1–76.

6. B. Bischoff, "Das griechische Element in der abendlaendischen Bildung des Mittelalters," *Byzantinische Zeitschrift* 44 (1951): 27–55; Louise R. Loomis, *Medieval Hellenism* (Lancaster, Pa., 1906); R. Weiss, "The Translators from the Greek of the Angevin Court of Naples," *Rinascimento* 1 (1950): 195–226; R. Weiss, "The Study of Greek in England during the Fourteenth Century," *Rinascimento,* 2 (1951): 209–239; Weiss, "The Greek Culture of South Italy in the Later Middle Ages," *Proceedings of the British Academy,* 37 (1951): 23–50; Weiss, "England and the Decree of the Council of Vienne on the Teaching of Greek, Arabic, Hebrew and Syriac," *Bibliothèque d'Humanisme et Renaissance,* 14 (1952): 1–9; Weiss, "Lo studio del greco all'abbazia di San Dionigi durante il medio evo," *Rivista di storia della chiesa in Italia,* 6 (1952): 426–438; Weiss, "Lo studio del greco all'Universita di Parigi," *Convivium,* N.S. 2 (1955): 146–149.

of a tradition of Greek studies in the West before the second half of the fourteenth century. In the inventories of medieval libraries Greek manuscripts are extremely rare, and in most instances what we find are bilingual Gospels or psalters. As to the translators from the Greek, we know that they acquired their knowledge of Greek and the Greek books from which they worked either in Sicily or in the East. Their knowledge of Greek was also quite limited, as we can see when we study their translations and collate them with the Greek originals. They translate "ad verbum" and without any feeling for the syntax or phraseology of classical Greek.[7] Also the content of their translations is narrowly limited. The translations cover almost exclusively the fields of theology, the sciences, and philosophy, and among the philosophical writings the works of Aristotle predominate. The other ancient Greek philosophers are represented only to a small extent, and the poets, orators, and historians of ancient Greece are practically omitted.[8] This choice, in what it includes and excludes, reflects in part a strong theological interest and in part a scientific interest of Arabic origin.[9] The interest that inspires these translations is didactic and scholastic. The translators choose treatises full of a content that may be learned and developed. That which was to characterize the humanists is completely absent: an interest for literature and for a thought that is diversified and fluid and a taste for the form and the nuances of language, of style, and of thought.

7. *Corpus Platonicum Medii Aevi, Plato Latinus,* ed. R. Klibansky, 4 vols. (London, 1940–1962). See my reviews in the *Journal of Philosophy,* 37 (1940): 695–697; 53 (1956): 196–201; 62 (1965): 14–17.

8. The main exceptions are Plato, Proclus, and Sextus Empiricus for the Greek philosophers not connected with the Aristotelian tradition and Demetrius (*de elocutione*) and Isocrates (*ad Demonicum*) for the rhetorical authors. Cf. Muckle, "Greek Works Translated into Latin;" Sabbadini, *Le Scoperte* (II 264, for Isocrates). None of these authors was completely translated during the Middle Ages.

9. M. Steinschneider, *Die Arabischen Uebersetzungen aus dem Griechischen* (Graz, 1960); R. Walzer, *Greek into Arabic* (Oxford, 1962); A. Badawi, *La transmission de la philosophie grecque au monde arabe* (Paris, 1968).

During the next period that goes from the middle of the four-teenth to the end of the sixteenth century, the state of Greek studies in Western Europe underwent a profound change. During the sixteenth century, the teaching of the classical Greek language and literature had become firmly established at the major universities and at many secondary schools. The chief Western libraries were full of Greek classical manuscripts, and a large part of the classical Greek texts had by then been widely distributed in printed edi-tions. All these Greek texts were translated into Latin and into the various national languages, either for the first time or in new and more accurate translations, and these translations had an even wider diffusion than the original texts themselves. There also developed a tradition of precise Greek scholarship which consti-tutes the first phase of Greek philology in the West and which finds expression not only in critical editions and translations of the texts, but also in commentaries and miscellaneous studies and in trea-tises on history and mythology, grammar and rhetoric, philosophy and theology.

This flourishing state of Greek studies in the West that sur-passed anything seen in that part of the world either in Roman antiquity or during the Middle Ages coincides in time with the decline and destruction of the Byzantine Empire and with the emigration of many Byzantine scholars to the West, and especially to Italy. Hence, there arises the question which is the subject of this paper: what was the contribution of the Byzantine tradition to the rich development of Greek studies that occurred in the West between the fourteenth and the sixteenth centuries and that was due in large part to the work of the Italian and other Western humanists?

In order to answer this question it would be necessary to study the history of classical scholarship during the Byzantine Middle Ages, a subject with which I am not well acquainted and which perhaps has not been sufficiently explored even by the specialists of Byzantine history. I must limit myself to a few well-established

facts, and perhaps they will be sufficient for our purpose. During
the long period that extends from the end of the eighth century
to the fourteenth and fifteenth, classical studies had their shorter or
longer periods of decline, to be sure, but they were never completely abandoned. We know that many classical texts were lost in
the period between the end of antiquity and the eighth century and
many others also after the eighth century. Yet, the greater part of
the Greek authors that we now have, with the exception of the
texts recently recovered by papyrologists, have been preserved
through the labors of Byzantine scholars. These texts were collected and kept in their libraries, they were recopied, read, and
studied. We also know that the classical poets and prose writers
were read in the schools at Constantinople and elsewhere at least
from the ninth century on, and it seems to be characteristic of the
Byzantine schools that the philosophers, both Plato and Aristotle,
and the Church Fathers were read together with Homer and the
tragedians, historians, and orators. As a matter of fact, we have
Byzantine commentaries and scholia not only on Aristotle and
Plato, but also on Homer, Pindar, and Sophocles, and these
commentaries and scholia that are based in part on the erudition
of the scholars of ancient Alexandria have been utilized by modern
classical scholars in their work on the same authors.

We must also keep in mind an important fact concerning the
history of the Greek language. Just as it happened with Latin in
the West, the spoken language of the Byzantine Middle Ages for
many centuries had moved far away from classical Greek, whether
Attic or Hellenistic, and a student who wanted to read the classical
authors had to learn first the grammar and vocabulary of classical
Greek. And just as in the Latin West, there was in the East a
continuous tradition of using as a literary language not the spoken
or popular language but classical Greek, or at least a classicizing
Greek resembling that of antiquity. Hence, the study of the classics
was not merely prompted by historical or literary curiosity, but
also by the practical requirements of linguistic and literary imita-

tion. Thus, we find handbooks of Greek grammar composed by Byzantine scholars for the use of students, whose spoken language was no longer classical Greek. It is, therefore, not a mere coincidence if the most important dictionaries of ancient Greek belong to the Byzantine period. The Byzantine scholars were also critical editors of classical texts in the proper sense of the word, and it is sufficient to cite the *Anthologia Palatina* or the *Bibliotheca* of Photios to remind us that we owe to these editions the preservation and transmission of these texts or at least of their summaries. If we add the textual criticism that is embodied in the Byzantine manuscripts and commentaries, and the historical, mythological, and rhetorical erudition that appears in the encyclopedias, it becomes obvious that Byzantine scholarship, with all its limitations, represents a flourishing and important period in the history of Greek studies and that the West had nothing comparable to offer either at the time of Roman antiquity or during the Latin Middle Ages. Moreover, in spite of its political decline and the continuous losses of important territories, the Byzantine Empire witnessed during its last centuries, and especially during the fourteenth century, a revival rather than a decline of classical studies. A large number of the best-known Byzantine scholars belong precisely to this late period. It is during that same period that we may notice for the first time a Western influence. Several Latin authors such as Cicero, Ovid, St. Augustine, and Boethius were translated into Greek for the first time, and some of these translations were made by authors such as Maximos Planudes, who was also one of the most learned students of classical Greek literature.[10]

If we keep in mind this flourishing state of philological studies in the East, we can easily understand why the Italian humanists, when they began to be interested in ancient Greek literature, had to turn toward Byzantium in order to obtain the texts and also the

10. For translations of Planudes, see Krumbacher, *Geschichte der byzantinischen Literatur,* pp. 544–546. For the Greek translations of St. Augustine, see M. Rackl, "Die griechischen Augustinusuebersetzungen," in *Miscellanea Francesco Ehrle,* 1 (Studi e Testi 37, Rome, 1924): 1–38.

linguistic and philological knowledge required for reading and understanding them. We know of the first attempts made by Petrarch, who took Greek lessons from Barlaam of Calabria and acquired Greek manuscripts of Homer and Plato,[11] and of Boccaccio, who took Leonzio Pilato into his house and made him teach Greek in Florence and translate Homer into Latin.[12] Even more important was the arrival in Italy of Manuel Chrysoloras and his activity as a teacher in Florence and elsewhere.[13] Among his pupils he counted some of the best humanists and Greek scholars of the early fifteenth century, and in spite of the short duration of his stay, his teaching had a lasting effect. This is attested to by the vast diffusion of the Greek grammar, which he composed for his Italian students, and by the work of his pupils; for example, the translation of Plato's *Republic* made by Uberto Decembrio and suggested and perhaps begun by Chrysoloras himself. With Chrysoloras begins, more than half a century before the fall of Constantinople, the exodus of Byzantine scholars to Italy, a movement that was to continue without interruption for several decades

11. E. H. Wilkins, *Life of Petrarch* (Chicago, 1961), pp. 33–34 and 136; G. Gentile, "Le traduzioni medievali di Platone e Francesco Petrarca," in his *Studi sul Rinascimento* (Florence, 1936), pp. 23–88. Petrarch's manuscript of the medieval Latin version of Plato's *Phaedo* has been identified as Paris. lat. 6567 A by L. Minio Paluello (*Plato Latinus,* Vol. II [London, 1950], p. xii). Petrarch's Greek manuscript of Homer has been identified as Ambr. J 98 inf. by Agostino Pertusi (*Leonzio Pilato fra Petrarca e Boccaccio* [Venice and Rome, 1964], pp. 62–72), Petrarch's Greek Plato more tentatively as Paris. gr. 1807 by E. Pellegrin (*La Bibliothèque des Visconti et des Sforza, Ducs de Milan, au XV e siècle* [Paris, 1955], p. 310; cf. Pertusi, *Leonzio Pilato fra Petrarca e Boccaccio,* p. 18).

12. A. Pertusi, *Leonzio Pilato fra Petrarca e Boccaccio.* The fact that Pilato did not merely tutor Boccaccio but also was appointed by the city authorities of Florence *"ad docendam grammaticam grecam et licteras grecas"* and received a salary from 1360 to 1362 has been recently documented by Gene A. Brucker ("Florence and Its University, 1348–1434," in *Action and Conviction in Early Modern Europe, Essays in Memory of E. H. Harbison,* ed. Theodore K. Rabb and Jerrold E. Seigel [Princeton, 1969], pp. 220–236 at pp. 231–233).

13. G. Cammelli, *I dotti bizantini e le origini dell'umanesimo,* 3 vols. (Florence, 1941–1954).

and to increase first with the Council of Ferrara and Florence in 1438 and then with the catastrophe of 1453.[14] But with Chryso-loras there also begins a movement in the opposite direction. When he returned from Italy to Constantinople, he was accompanied by several Italian pupils, including Guarino. From that time on until the end of the Byzantine Empire and even afterwards under the Turkish rule, there was a steady traveling of Italian humanists to Constantinople and to other Greek cities. We find among them some of the best Greek scholars of the age: Aurispa, Tortelli, and above all Francesco Filelfo, who married the daughter of his Byzantine teacher and who was one of the few Italian humanists capable of writing letters and even poems in classical Greek.[15]

When we speak of the Greek journeys of Guarino, Filelfo, and many others, we usually stress the fact that they learned Greek and brought back an important number of classical Greek manuscripts. We should add that they also learned from their Byzantine masters the philological method that enabled them to read, to understand, and to translate the ancient texts. The same is true of the Byzan-tine scholars beginning with Chrysoloras himself, who came to teach in Florence, in Padua, and at the other Italian and European universities. They imparted to their Western students not only the Greek classical language that was a learned and not a spoken language, but also the method of interpreting the classical texts as it had been developed in the Byzantine philological tradition. I am convinced that the selection of the Greek authors that were read by the students, and even the choice and sequence of the texts of the preferred authors as they were read was transmitted in this manner from the Byzantine to the Western schools.[16] To give an example, the reading of Aristophanes always began with the *Plutos* and that

14. For the later period, see Deno J. Geanakoplos, *Greek Scholars in Venice* (Cambridge, Mass., 1960).

15. Sabbadini, *Le Scoperte* I, 43–71; E. W. Bodnar, *Cyriacus of Ancona and Athens* (Bruxelles, 1960).

16. This idea was first suggested to me by James Hutton.

of Euripides with the *Hecuba,* and aside from the obvious reasons of facility and decency, there was also an element of school tradition. There is also a certain conception of learning that is reflected not only in the choice of the authors and texts to be read, but also in the grouping and connection of the subjects taught. The idea that poets and prose writers should form the subjects of different courses is also expressed in the school curriculum of the Latin Middle Ages, but the tendency to treat the philosophers, especially Plato but also Aristotle and the Patristic authors, together with the poets and orators was characteristic of the Byzantine school and seems to have influenced the Greek and perhaps even the Latin scholarship of the Renaissance humanists. I am inclined to think that the learning of the Renaissance humanists, in the extent and limitations of their interests as well as in their attitude toward the texts they studied had closer links with the Byzantine didactic tradition than with that of medieval scholasticism. These are rather minute observations, and at the present state of our knowledge they are hard to prove. Yet, I am convinced that they should and will be investigated as soon as our bibliographical knowledge of manuscripts and printed texts and our documentary knowledge of the universities and other schools will have become more complete than it is at present.

The fourteenth century saw only the first beginnings of Greek scholarship in Italy, whereas the fifteenth and sixteenth centuries brought about the full development of Greek philology in the West, a development that was largely due to the influence of Byzantine philology and of Italian humanism. Let us briefly indicate the diffusion of Greek learning during the Renaissance in its various aspects, and let us begin with the schools. During the first half of the fifteenth century, the teaching of Greek was still quite sporadic even at the major universities, but during the second half of the century, it became more or less continuous, and during the sixteenth century, it spread also outside of Italy. Among the teachers of Greek we encounter several Byzantine scholars of

fame: Theodore Gaza at Ferrara, John Argyropoulos at Florence
and Rome, Demetrios Chalcondylas at Padua, Florence, and
Pavia, Constantine Lascaris at Messina, and Marcus Musurus at
Venice and Padua, to mention only some of the most famous
masters. Yet, already during the first half of the fifteenth century,
we find also Italian humanists among the teachers of Greek, above
all the direct or indirect pupils of the Byzantine masters, for
example, Guarino at Venice and Ferrara, Filelfo at Bologna,
Florence, and Milan, Poliziano at Florence. We should add a
number of other scholars who have been less studied but probably
were quite learned, such as Lianoro Lianori, who taught Greek at
Bologna and knew it well enough to write letters in Greek.[17]
Greek instruction obviously began with the elementary study of
Greek grammar, and we have numerous manuscript and printed
copies of Greek grammars, from the Byzantine grammar of
Moschopoulos to the small treatises written by the Greek pro-
fessors, for example, Chrysoloras, Gaza, and Constantine Lascaris,
for their Italian pupils. We are not so well informed about the
Greek authors selected for reading since the school documents are
usually not explicit enough, whereas the texts of introductory lectures, of courses, and of commentaries are rare and have not yet
been much studied. It appears that Homer and Plato, Xenophon,
and Demosthenes were among the favorite authors. It is probable,
at least for the fifteenth century, that some of the translations from
the Greek were school products and also were used to help other
beginning students. The introductory lectures given by Chalcondylas at Padua have been preserved by a German student,[18] and
we also have some of the introductory lectures given by Argyropoulos in Florence.[19] A manuscript based on the Paduan

17. Some Greek letters of Lianoro to Tortelli are found in the well-
known ms. Vat. lat. 3908.
18. The manuscript will be studied and published by Prof. D. J.
Geanakoplos.
19. K. Muellner, *Reden und Briefe italienischer Humanisten* (Vienna,
1899), pp. 3–56.

lectures of Gregoropoulos has been preserved in Germany and has recently been studied, and thus we learn the important fact that he also lectured on Aristophanes and the tragedians.[20] We may expect further details from Greek manuscripts that carry Latin glosses or translations and from Latin manuscripts that contain Greek notes. For example, I studied some years ago the manuscript of Aristotle's *Ethics* and *Politics,* now preserved in New York, that was used by Ermolao Barbaro for his courses at Padua.[21] I was able to show that he did not work from the Greek text or from Bruni's Latin version, as had often been assumed, but from the medieval translations. On the other hand, it is apparent from Ermolao's glosses that he did use the Greek text and Bruni's version to correct the Latin text that he was supposed to explain to his students.

Equally important and perhaps more thoroughly studied are the problems connected with the Greek books and the libraries of the Renaissance period. The fifteenth and sixteenth centuries saw not only the migration of the Byzantine scholars to the West, but also the exodus of many Greek manuscripts to the Western countries. The Byzantine scholars who went to Italy brought their books with them, and the Italian humanists who went to Greece returned to Italy with Greek manuscripts and sometimes with entire libraries of Greek manuscripts. Italian princes and patrons began to collect Greek manuscripts. They bought the manuscripts brought from Greece by scholars, monks, and merchants, and even sent scholars to Greece for the sole purpose of acquiring manuscripts. The best-known example is the mission of John Lascaris for Lorenzo de'

---

20. Berlin, ms. lat. oct. 374. See H. Meyer, "Ein Kollegheft des Humanisten Cono," *Zentralblatt fuer Bibliothekswesen,* 53 (1936): 281–284; A. Oleroff, "L'Humaniste dominicain Jean Conon et le Crétois Jean Grégoropoulos," *Scriptorium,* 4 (1950): 104–107. For another manuscript of Cono, see Sister Agnes Clare Way, "Gregorius Nazianzenus," in *Catalogus Translationum et Commentariorum,* Vol. II, ed. P. O. Kristeller and F. E. Cranz (Washington, D.C., 1971), pp. 43–192 at 113 and 142–143.
21. P. O. Kristeller, *Studies in Renaissance Thought and Letters* (Rome, 1956), pp. 337–353.

Medici that occurred several decades after the Turkish conquest.[22] Still in the sixteenth century, Francesco Patrizi collected Greek manuscripts in Cyprus and elsewhere and subsequently resold them to Philip II of Spain.[23] In other words, the trade in Greek manuscripts did not stop with the fall of Constantinople, and we should remember that after 1453 several areas of Greek speech and civilization, such as Euboea and Morea, Cyprus, Rhodes, and Crete, remained for shorter or longer periods under Venetian rule. The core of the great collections of Greek manuscripts in Europe goes back to the fifteenth and sixteenth centuries: the Laurentian and Vatican libraries and the Marciana, which had for its first nucleus the collection of Bessarion, were formed in the fifteenth century; the collections in Paris, the Escorial, Munich and Vienna in the sixteenth century; those in Oxford and Leyden shortly afterwards. Still at the present time the editor of ancient Greek texts must use the manuscripts in these libraries, as well as those that are still in the libraries of Greece and of the other Eastern countries that have or had close ties with the Greek Church and with Greek culture, such as Russia and Turkey. The Western collections of Greek manuscripts contain not only manuscripts written in Greece and later brought to the West. There are also some manuscripts written in Greek Italy and Sicily during the Middle Ages and a large number of manuscripts that were copied in the West itself from older manuscripts, as we learn from the dates and colophons of the manuscripts. They were mostly written by exiled Byzantine scholars who made their livings as copyists but also

22. K. K. Mueller, "Neue Mittheilungen ueber Janos Lascaris und die Mediceische Bibliothek," *Centralblatt fuer Bibliothekswesen*, 1 (1884): 332–412; B. Knös, *Un ambassadeur de l'hellénisme, Janus Lascaris, et la tradition gréco-byzantine dans l'humanisme français* (Uppsala and Paris, 1945).

23. E. Jacobs, "Francesco Patricio und seine Sammlung griechischer Handschriften in der Bibliothek des Escorial," *Zentralblatt fuer Bibliothekswesen*, 25 (1908): 19–47; J.-Th. Papademetriou, "The Sources and the Character of *Del Governo de' Regni*," *Transactions and Proceedings of the American Philological Association*, 92 (1961): 422–439 at 434–437.

often by Western scholars who copied the Greek texts for their own use. We have Greek manuscripts copied or annotated by Poliziano, Ficino, Ermolao Barbaro, and even by Leonardo Bruni.[24] In spite of their relatively recent date, these Greek manuscripts copied by Byzantine or Italian scholars are important for the history and emendation of the texts, and in some instances where we have no older manuscripts these late copies must even serve as the basis for editing the text. The Greek manuscripts also reflect the influence of the Byzantine tradition in the field of paleography. The majority of our Greek manuscripts was written in Byzantine minuscule, a script that was in general use for literary texts from the ninth century on. This was the script still used by the Byzantine scholars of the fifteenth century and adopted and imitated by the Italian and other Western scholars when they learned to write Greek. This Byzantine minuscule is the basis of the Greek characters used by Aldus and the other printers and publishers of Greek texts in the sixteenth century, just as the Roman and Italic characters used by the early printers are based on the two humanistic scripts commonly used in the Latin manuscript books of fifteenth-century Italy. Aside from certain conventional abbreviations and ligatures that have been abandoned in more recent times, the Byzantine minuscule is still the recognizable

24. For Poliziano, see *Mostra del Poliziano, Catalogo,* ed. T. Lodi and A. Perosa (Florence, 1955). For Ficino, see M. Sicherl, "Neuentdeckte Handschriften von Marsilio Ficino und Johannes Reuchlin," *Scriptorium,* 16 (1962): 50–61; P. O. Kristeller, "Some Original Letters and Autograph Manuscripts of Marsilio Ficino," in *Studi di Bibliografia e di Storia in Onore di Tammaro De Marinis,* Vol. 3 (Verona and Vatican City, 1964), pp. 5–33. For Ermolao Barbaro, see above. For Leonardo Bruni, see C. Stornaiolo, *Codices Urbinates Graeci Bibliothecae Vaticanae* (Rome, 1895), p. 38 (cod. 32); p. 39 (cod. 33); p. 48 (cod. 42); pp. 149–150 (cod. 97); Sotheby & Co., *Catalogue of Nineteen Highly Distinguished Medieval and Renaissance Manuscripts . . . The Property of Sir Sydney Cockerell . . .* (London, April 3, 1957), p. 15, no. 10, where the opinion of Miss Barbour is cited. The manuscript was reportedly acquired by Mr. Martin Bodmer (Genève-Cologny), but an enquiry which I addressed to Mr. Bodmer obtained only an evasive reply.

source for the printed characters used in our modern editions of the Greek classics.

This last observation leads us to another important factor in the diffusion of Greek learning during the Renaissance, that is, to printing. The first Greek classical texts were printed in Florence and Milan, but very soon, through Aldus and other learned printers both Greek and Italian, Venice became the most active center of Greek printing. She later had to share this place with Paris, Antwerp, and Leyden, just as she shared her predominance in the field of Latin printing with Lyons and Basel.[25] Erasmus went to Venice and to the printing shop of Aldus when he wanted to enhance his knowledge of Greek, a very significant episode that has been properly emphasized in recent studies. Within the vast output of the presses during the late fifteenth and sixteenth centuries, Greek books constituted but a small percentage, but their distribution is a decisive element for the history of advanced learning during the period. We may say without exaggeration that in the course of the sixteenth century almost all the important texts of ancient Greece that had been preserved by the Byzantine Middle Ages had become accessible to Western scholars, both through the manuscripts of the major Western libraries and through the printed editions published by the great Hellenists of the period that found their place also in the more modest libraries of schools and of private scholars.

If we want to understand the diffusion of Greek literature during the Renaissance, we must also take into consideration the translations into Western languages, and especially into Latin. Even during the sixteenth century, when Greek learning was more widely diffused in the West than ever before, the scholars who knew Greek and knew it well constituted only a minority, whereas

---

25. *La stampa greca a Venezia nei secoli XV e XVI, Catalogo di Mostra,* ed. M. Finazzi (Venice, 1968).

Latin was known more or less well by every person who had received a humanistic or university education. Hence, it is quite understandable that the Latin translations of the Greek authors, either by themselves or along with the Greek text, had a much wider diffusion than the original Greek texts themselves.[26] Whereas the diffusion of the original Greek texts was a completely new fact and never occurred during the Middle Ages, Latin translations from the Greek were by no means unknown during the Middle Ages, as we have seen before. If we wish to define the difference between the Middle Ages and the Renaissance in this area, we must stress two different facets of the question. In the case of those Greek texts that had been known before through medieval Latin translations, it would be necessary to compare the new humanistic translations of the same texts with the earlier ones. Curiously enough, such a comparison between the medieval and humanistic translations and the corresponding Greek originals has not yet been attempted, and, hence, our judgment on the relative merits of these translations must remain rather tentative. We may concede to some admirers of the Middle Ages that some humanistic translations, such as Bruni's versions of Aristotle, are rather free and do not sufficiently insist on a precise and consistent terminology. On the other hand, after having examined the medieval versions of Plato and Proclus, I am convinced that the

26. For the case of Alexander of Aphrodisias and a few other authors, see *Catalogus Translationum et Commentariorum,* I–II, ed. P. O. Kristeller (Washington, D.C., 1960–1971), especially the article by F. E. Cranz (I:77–135; II:411–422). For the translations of Aristotle, see *Aristoteles Latinus,* ed. G. Lacombe and others, 3 vols. (Rome, 1939–Bruges and Paris, 1961); E. Garin, "Le traduzioni umanistiche di Aristotele nel secolo XV," *Atti e Memorie dell'Accademia Fiorentina di Scienze Morali "La Colombaria,"* 16 (N.S. 2, 1947–1950): 55–104. For the translations of Plato, see *Plato Latinus,* ed. Klibansky; Klibansky, *The Continuity of the Platonic Tradition during the Middle Ages* (London, 1939 and 1950); E. Garin, "Ricerche sulle traduzioni di Platone nella prima metà del secolo XV," in *Medioevo e Rinascimento, Studi in onore di Bruno Nardi,* I (Florence, 1955): 339–374.

humanists had a more advanced knowledge of classical Greek than had their medieval predecessors, both of its vocabulary and of its syntax, phraseology, and style.[27] We must also note that the vast enterprise of translating the classical Greek authors into Latin was carried out not only by Italian and other Western Hellenists, but also by many Byzantine scholars who had acquired enough Latin learning for the purpose, such as George of Trebisond, Gaza, Argyropoulos, and Bessarion himself to whom we owe some translations of Aristotle and Xenophon. The rivalry between medieval and humanistic translations poses a number of problems, especially for Aristotle and for some scientific authors such as Hippocrates, Galen, Archimedes, and Ptolemy. We do not yet know precisely to what extent humanist translators utilized earlier translations when available and to what extent they succeeded in replacing the work of their medieval predecessors.[28] We know that in some instances the humanistic and the medieval translations lived far into the late sixteenth century in a kind of coexistence and were used simultaneously by teachers and scholars, but we also know that the medieval translations when copied or printed during the fifteenth and sixteenth centuries were often subjected to more or less extensive revisions. The bibliography and textual history of these translations leaves room for much further study, and it is a subject of great importance. For it is important to know what impact the new translations, with their changed terminology and interpretation, had on the understanding of the basic philosophical and scientific texts and, hence, on the philosophical and scientific thought itself, which was still to a large extent formulated through

27. For the *Plato Latinus,* see note 7. Procli Diadochi *Tria Opuscula,* ed. H. Boese (Berlin, 1960); see my review in the *Journal of Philosophy,* 59 (1962): 74–78.

28. For an important example, see J. Soudek, "The Genesis and Tradition of Leonardo Bruni's Annotated Latin Version of the (Pseudo-) Aristotelian 'Economics,'" *Scriptorium,* 12 (1958): 260–268; Soudek, "Leonardo Bruni and His Public: A Statistical and Interpretative Study of His Annotated Latin Version of the (Pseudo-) Aristotelian Economics," *Studies in Medieval and Renaissance History,* 5 (1968): 49–136.

the interpretation of these texts.[29] The same consideration holds
for the new translations of the Bible and of the Greek Church
Fathers and for their influence on the theological thought of the
period.

Even more obvious and perhaps more important is the humanist
contribution in the case of those Greek texts which had never been
translated into Latin during the Middle Ages. The volume and
importance of these texts seems to have been greatly underesti-
mated by many historians who have studied the problem. They
include even a few texts of the *Corpus Aristotelicum,* such as the
Mechanics (and in a way the *Poetics*) and a large number of
Greek commentaries on Aristotle,[30] as well as many writings of
the same scientific authors that had been known to the Middle
Ages through some of their works, such as Hippocrates, Galen,
Archimedes, and Ptolemy.[31] Moreover, there are other ancient
philosophers besides Aristotle of whom the Middle Ages knew
only some works, as Plato, Sextus, and Proclus; or nothing at all,
such as Epicurus, Epictetus, or Plotinus; and, if we include the
more popular and more widely read authors, Xenophon, Plutarch,
or Lucian. If we turn to Greek literature in the proper sense of the
word, everything was new and unknown from the Western point of
view: Lysias, Isocrates, Demosthenes, and the other orators;
Herodotus, Thucydides and Polybius; Homer and Hesiod; the
tragedians and Aristophanes; Pindar and the other lyrical poets,
not to mention the Anthology of the Greek epigrams or many

29. A vast bibliography of Greek and Latin editions of Aristotle published in the fifteenth and sixteenth centuries is being prepared by Prof.
F. Edward Cranz.

30. P. O. Kristeller, *Studies,* pp. 340–342. P. L. Rose and S. Drake, "The
Pseudo-Aristotelian *Questions in Mechanics* in Renaissance Culture," *Studies
in the Renaissance,* 18 (1971): 65–104.

31. For Galen, see R. J. Durling, "A Chronological Census of Renaissance Editions and Translations of Galen," *Journal of the Warburg and
Courtauld Institutes,* 24 (1961): 230–305. For the Geography of Ptolemy,
see D. Durand, "Tradition and Innovation in Fifteenth Century Italy, 'Il
primato dell'Italia' in the Field of Science," *Journal of the History of Ideas,*
4 (1943): 1–20 at p. 4.

lesser poets and prose writers. In other words, an educated person of the sixteenth century, whether he was able to read Greek or not, had at his disposal the complete patrimony of classical Greek literature and science. For anybody who appreciates Greek literature and non-Aristotelian Greek philosophy, this is a cultural development of the very first order, and it is a fact of which we must remind those numerous historians who insist on the essentially medieval character of humanism and of the Renaissance. It is to this increased availability of Greek texts brought about under the influence of humanism that we owe at least in part the great literary wealth of the Renaissance and of modern times and the greater variety of modern philosophical ideas as compared to the more rigid and more limited alternatives of medieval Aristotelianism. In the scientific disciplines it was necessary to absorb and digest the advanced mathematical, astronomical, and medical texts of ancient Greece before their conclusions could be surpassed. In these fields the quarrel of the ancients and moderns and the idea of progress could not have made their appearance before the sixteenth century.

If the heritage of ancient Greek culture in all its aspects still constitutes an essential part of our present civilization, in spite of the additions and transformations brought about by later centuries, we are indebted for it to the Italian and other Western humanists of the Renaissance and to their Byzantine predecessors. We must also remember another more limited but no less essential contribution that the scholars of the Renaissance have transmitted to later centuries: Greek philology which includes textual criticism, the method of interpretation, and the method of historical and antiquarian research. This philology passed from the Byzantine scholars to the Italian humanists and from the latter to the French and Dutch philologists of the sixteenth century, and to the English and German and finally to the American scholars of more recent times. Each age and country added something new to the common tradition, and we should like to think that the methods of research have been steadily improved and refined in the course of the centuries and that they have proved their validity also when applied to the study of languages and cultures other than those of classical antiquity.

For two reasons, then, for the continuing impact of Greek literature and culture on modern Western civilization and for the impulse given to classical, philological, and historical studies, Byzantine and Italian humanism, different and also connected, have a lasting importance in the history of European civilization. Hence, it should be worthwhile to explore these rich and interesting movements much further, especially in those aspects that have not yet been properly investigated or understood.

5. Byzantine and Western Platonism in the Fifteenth Century

The history of Byzantine and Western Platonism is an important subject and one that has not been neglected by intellectual historians, but it is somewhat difficult and complicated, and many of its facets have not yet been sufficiently explored, as far as I can judge. We have a certain number of recent monographs on the major representatives of Byzantine and Italian Platonism,[1] but several lesser figures who had a significant part in the intellectual development of the period remain comparatively unknown. Moreover, we still lack a comprehensive and documented history of Renaissance Platonism, and there is no modern history of the controversy about the superiority of Plato and Aristotle.[2] In other

1. Milton V. Anastos, "Pletho's Calendar and Liturgy," *Dumbarton Oaks Papers,* 4 (1948): 183–305. F. Masai, *Pléthon et le Platonisme de Mistra* (Paris, 1956). L. Mohler, *Kardinal Bessarion als Theologe, Humanist und Staatsmann,* 3 vols. (Paderborn, 1923–1942). P. O. Kristeller, *Il pensiero filosofico di Marsilio Ficino* (Florence, 1953). E. Garin, *Giovanni Pico della Mirandola* (Florence, 1937). *L'opera e il pensiero di Giovanni Pico della Mirandola nella storia dell'Umanesimo,* 2 vols. (Florence, 1965). B. Kieszkowski, *Studi sul Platonismo del Rinascimento in Italia* (Florence, 1936).

2. B. Tatakis, *La philosophie byzantine* (Paris, 1949), pp. 281–314. Cf. Boivin, "Querelle des philosophes du quinzième siecle," *Mémoires de Litéra-*

words, we know to some extent the thought of Plethon and Bessarion, of Ficino and Pico. But aside from many aspects of the thought of these authors that remain still obscure or doubtful, we do not yet know the precise links that connect them with each other or with other earlier or later thinkers, and their sources and influences are still to a large extent unknown to us. Instead of trying to give a synthesis that would seem premature at this stage, I prefer to admit the preliminary character of our knowledge, and especially of my knowledge of the subject, and to indicate as clearly as possible the problems that are still in need of further investigation.

If we read some of the textbooks of the history of philosophy, we shall usually find them saying (or at least they did so until a few years ago) that the contrast between medieval and Renaissance thought in the West may be roughly described as a contrast between Aristotelianism and Platonism. Medieval scholastic thought was dominated by "the master of those who know,"[3] whereas the Renaissance discovered "Plato who in that group came closest to the goal that may be reached by those whom heaven favors."[4] This simple and pleasant formula has been demolished, as it happens, by the more detailed research of recent historians. We have learned that there was also during the Middle Ages a more or less continuous Platonist current[5] and, on the other hand, that the Aristotelian school remained very strong throughout the sixteenth century and even underwent some of its most characteristic developments during that very period.[6] Yet, in

ture tirés des registres de l'Académie Royale des Inscriptions et Belles-Lettres, 3 (1772): 531–554. None of these accounts is adequate or complete.

3. *Inferno*, IV:131.

4. *Trionfo della Fama*, III:4–6. Cf. P. O. Kristeller, *Eight Philosophers of the Italian Renaissance* (Stanford, 1964), p. 169.

5. R. Klibansky, *The Continuity of the Platonic Tradition during the Middle Ages* (London, 1939).

6. B. Nardi, *Saggi sull'aristotelismo padovano dal secolo XIV al XVI* (Florence, 1958). J. H. Randall, *The School of Padua and the Emergence*

this as in other cases, we should not push revisionism to the utmost extreme. Renaissance Platonism remains, after all, an established fact, and we are still confronted with the task of understanding and explaining it. Cusanus, Ficino, and Pico were the most vigorous thinkers of the fifteenth century, and their influence during their own time and during the subsequent centuries was powerful, although it is somewhat hard to describe, especially if we think exclusively in terms of academic and institutional traditions. Moreover, when we use the term "Platonism," we should not treat it as a fixed and rigid category. We must realize that under this label we may expect to find in each instance a different combination of ideas and doctrines that remains to be identified and explained. We also should admit that the name and authority of Plato covers at the same time the vast tradition of ancient and later Neoplatonism and that for the very reason that people considered Platonism as a kind of perennial philosophy (the term was invented by a Platonizing bishop of the sixteenth century, Agostino Steuco),[7] they were also tempted to associate with it many philosophical, theological, and scientific ideas that had a very different origin.

If we wish to understand the development of Platonism during the Renaissance, we must go back for a moment to Roman antiquity and to the Latin Middle Ages. We find traces of Platonic and Platonist influences in some of the philosophical and rhetorical works of Cicero, who even translated a part of Plato's *Timaeus*.[8] The philosophical treatises of Apuleius are among the most important preserved sources for that school of ancient philosophy which

---

of Modern Science (Padua, 1961). P. O. Kristeller, *La tradizione aristotelica nel Rinascimento* (Padua, 1962); "Renaissance Aristotelianism," *Greek-Roman and Byzantine Studies,* 6 (1965): 157–174.

7. Charles B. Schmitt, "Perennial Philosophy," *Journal of the History of Ideas,* 27 (1966): 505–532. Cf. below, p. 153.

8. The most Platonist passages are found in the *Somnium Scipionis,* in the *Tusculan Disputations,* and in the *Orator.* The translation of the *Timaeus* covers 27d–37c, 38c–43b, 46b–47b of the text.

has recently come to be known as Middle Platonism.[9] Apuleius was also the reputed translator of the dialogue *Asclepius,* the only complete source of Hermetism known to Western readers throughout the Middle Ages.[10] In late antiquity the knowledge of Plato was strengthened by Calcidius' partial translation and commentary of the *Timaeus,* a work whose tremendous influence we can appreciate only now that we have an adequate critical edition of it.[11] The Neoplatonism of Plotinus and his school had its repercussions also in the Latin West. Aside from Victorinus and Macrobius,[12] we must mention especially St. Augustine, whose philosophical thought was much more deeply influenced by Plato and Plotinus than some of his recent theological interpreters are inclined to admit,[13] and Boethius, whose widely read *Consolation of Philosophy* shows the impact of the same school. Compared with these strong elements of Platonism, the traces of Aristotle in the philosophical literature of Latin antiquity are rather meager. We note primarily a certain acquaintance with Aristotelian logic in Cicero and Augustine and, above all, in Boethius, who translated the first two treatises of the *Organon,* along with the Neoplatonist Porphyry's Introduction to the first treatise, and probably also the remaining parts of the same collection.[14]

Thus, we may easily understand why medieval philosophy and theology up to the twelfth century followed a strong Neoplatonic

9. Apuleius, *De deo Socratis; De Platone et eius dogmate.* Cf. W. Theiler, *Die Vorbereitung des Neuplatonismus* (Berlin, 1930).

10. *Hermès Trismégiste,* ed. A. D. Nock and A. J. Festugière, Vol. II (Paris, 1945), pp. 296–355.

11. (Platonis) *Timaeus a Calcidio translatus commentarioque instructus* (*Corpus Platonicum Medii Aevi,* ed. R. Klibansky, *Plato Latinus* IV), ed. J. H. Waszink (London and Leyden, 1962). The translation extends to p. 53c of the text.

12. For Victorinus, see now his *Traités théologiques sur la Trinité,* 2 vols., ed. P. Henry and P. Hadot (Paris, 1960).

13. Cf. P. O. Kristeller, *Studies in Renaissance Thought and Letters* (Rome, 1956), pp. 355–372.

14. *Aristoteles Latinus,* ed. G. Lacombe and others, *Codices,* 3 vols. (Rome, 1939– Bruges, 1961).

trend, whereas the influence of Aristotle was felt almost exclusively in the field of logic, especially after all treatises of the
Organon had become generally known. Yet, the twelfth century
also saw the beginning of that intellectual revolution that was to
bear fruit during the following two centuries. In the vast number of
philosophical and scientific texts which were then translated for
the first time from Greek and Arabic into Latin,[15] the most
important philosophical texts were those of Aristotle and his
commentators. Thus, the West acquired the entire, or almost the
entire, *Corpus* of Aristotle's preserved writings, along with many
of their commentaries. When the new universities in the thirteenth
century introduced a systematic instruction in the philosophical
disciplines, and especially in logic and natural philosophy, the
writings of Aristotle were naturally adopted as the main textbooks,
a function for which they were eminently suitable on account of
the completeness of their coverage and the precision and consistency of their method and terminology. The Aristotelianism of the
universities, as it developed in the thirteenth and fourteenth centuries and continued, although with gradually diminishing importance, through the Renaissance down to the eighteenth century,
was not so much a compact system of uniform doctrines as a
diversified tradition of teaching based on a common terminology
and a common set of topics and problems. The translators of the
twelfth and thirteenth centuries did not entirely forget the writings
of the Platonist school. There were translations of Plato's *Meno*
and *Phaedo* by the Sicilian Henricus Aristippus and several translations of Proclus by the Flemish Dominican William of Moerbeke,[16] translations which had a demonstrable impact on the

15. M. Steinschneider, *Die europaeischen Uebersetzungen aus dem
Arabischen* (repr. Graz, 1956). J. T. Muckle, "Greek Works Translated
Directly into Latin before 1350," *Mediaeval Studies*, 4 (1942): 33–42; 5
(1943): 102–114.
16. *Plato Latinus* I-III (*Meno interprete Henrico Aristippo*, ed. V.
Kordeuter and C. Labowsky [London, 1940]; *Phaedo interprete Henrico
Aristippo*, ed. L. Minio Paluello [London, 1950]: *Parmenides usque ad*

mystical writers and even on Thomas Aquinas.[17] But without forgetting these exceptions, it remains a basic fact that the academic and scientific philosophy of the Latin West during the later Middle Ages was dominated by the writings of Aristotle in a manner that had its precedent among the Arabs but was entirely different from the traditions of Greek and Roman antiquity and, as we shall see, of the Byzantines.

The preoccupations of the new humanist movement that asserted itself in contrast to the scholastic tradition were in part literary and scholarly, to be sure, but in part also philosophical and, especially, moral. With Petrarch the rebellion against scholasticism took the form of praising Plato above Aristotle, although Plato and his works were still comparatively unknown. This attitude appears not only in the *Triumph of Fame* from which I quoted a few lines,[18] but also in the treatise *On his own and other people's ignorance* that was based on a controversy Petrarch had with some friends in Venice.[19] In this, as in so many other ways, we may call Petrarch a prophet of the later Renaissance who

---

finem primae hypothesis necnon Procli Commentarium in Parmenidem, Pars ultima adhuc inedita interprete Guillelmo de Moerbeka, ed. R. Klibansky and C. Labowsky [London, 1953]). *Procli Diadochi Tria Opuscula,* ed. H. Boese [Berlin, 1960]. Proclus, *The Elements of Theology,* ed. E. R. Dodds, 2d ed. [Oxford, 1963]. "Procli Elementatio Theologica translata a Guilelmo de Moerbeke," ed. C. Vansteenkiste, *Tijdschrift voor Philosophie,* 13 (1951): 263–301; 492–531. M. Grabmann, *Guglielmo di Moerbeke O.P.* (Rome, 1946).

17. C. Fabro, *Participation et causalité selon S. Thomas d'Aquin* (Louvain, 1961); *La nozione metafisica di partecipazione secondo S. Tommaso d'Aquino,* 3d ed. (Turin, 1963). P. O. Kristeller, *Le thomisme et la pensée italienne de la Renaissance* (Montreal, 1967). A commentary on Proclus' *Elements of Theology* by the Dominican Berthold of Moosburg is still unpublished.

18. See note 4 above.

19. *Renaissance Philosophy of Man,* ed. E. Cassirer and others (Chicago, 1948), pp. 47–133 (English translation by Hans Nachod). Cf. P. O. Kristeller, "Petrarch's 'Averroists,'" *Bibliothèque d'Humanisme et Renaissance,* 14 (1952): 59–65; "Il Petrarca, l'Umanesimo e la Scolastica a Venezia," in *La Civiltà Veneziana del Trecento* (Florence, 1956), pp. 147–178.

opened the way, as it were, that was to lead to the Plato translations of Bruni and of other humanists and to Ficino's first complete translation of Plato's works.[20]

But this new interest in Plato and his works did not turn
toward the Latin traditions of antiquity or the early Middle Ages,
but rather toward Byzantium, where the original texts of Plato and
of his school had been preserved and studied during those long
centuries when they had remained largely unknown in the West.
Petrarch already received from the Orient a Greek manuscript
containing some dialogues of Plato, and this was probably the first
Greek manuscript of Plato that came to the West since ancient
Roman times.[21] When the teaching of Greek in the West received
its first lasting impetus from Manuel Chrysoloras,[22] some of its
first fruits were the Plato translations made by his pupils, especially that of the *Republic* by Uberto Decembrio and that of the
Apology, Crito, Gorgias, and other works by Leonardo Bruni.[23]
When the Byzantine Platonist Gemistos Plethon came to the
Council of Ferrara and Florence in 1438 and 1439, he aroused so
much interest for Platonic philosophy among the Italian humanists
whom he met that Marsilio Ficino was able to say several decades
afterwards that it was the impression made by Plethon on Cosimo
de' Medici that led to the founding of his own Platonic Academy

20. E. Garin, "Ricerche sulle traduzioni di Platone nella prima metà
del sec. XV," in *Medioevo e Rinascimento, Studi in onore di Bruno Nardi,*
Vol. 1 (Florence, 1955), pp. 339–374. P. O. Kristeller, "Marsilio Ficino as
a Beginning Student of Plato," *Scriptorium,* 20 (1966–1967): 41–54.
21. Kristeller, *Renaissance Philosophy of Man,* p. 112. A. Pertusi,
Leonzio Pilato fra Petrarca e Boccaccio (Venice and Rome, 1964), p. 18.
22. We now know that Leontius Pilatus was appointed as lecturer of
Greek at the University of Florence 1360–1362, see Gene A. Brucker,
"Florence and Its University, 1384–1434," in *Action and Conviction in
Early Modern Europe, Essays in Memory of E. H. Harbison,* ed.
Theodore K. Rabb and Jerrold E. Seigel (Princeton, N.J., 1969), pp. 220–
236 at 231–232. For Leontius, see Pertusi, *Leonzio Pilato fra Petrarca e
Boccaccio.*
23. See note 20 above.

and to the revival of Platonism brought about by the activities of that Academy.[24]

These well-known facts prompt us to enquire about the fate of the Platonic writings and of the Platonic and Neoplatonic tradition in medieval Byzantium. Many details of the history of this tradition are still obscure, but a few facts may be easily summed up. When the Neoplatonic school of Athens, one of the last intellectual centers of ancient paganism, was closed by Justinian in 529, Simplicius and some of his colleagues went to Persia. Yet, it would be wrong to assume that these events marked the end of Platonism in the Byzantine world.[25] Simplicius returned after a short while to Greece, and most of his extant writings were composed after his return. Moreover, the Christian writers of the Greek East had absorbed for several centuries a strong dose of Platonist thought, as may be easily shown in the writings of Clement and Origen, Gregory of Nyssa, and the so-called Dionysius the Areopagite. We also know for sure that at least from the ninth century on Plato's works were copied, read, and studied in Constantinople and in the other cultural centers of the oriental empire. From that period on, the study of Plato and also of Aristotle remained an integral part of the Byzantine scholarly or, if we wish, humanistic tradition. That is, Plato was read and studied together with the poets and prose writers of classical antiquity. This seems to have been the type of scholarship that characterized the work of Archbishop Arethas for whom one of the earliest extant manuscripts of Plato was copied.[26] A Platonism of a more philosophical and specula-

24. Marsilius Ficinus, *Opera omnia,* Vol. II (Basel, 1576, repr. Turin, 1959), p. 1537.

25. Prof. Alan Cameron of Bedford College, London, questioned the enforcement of Justinian's decree in a paper that to my knowledge has not yet been published.

26. H. Alline, *Histoire du teœte de Platon* (Paris, 1915), esp. pp. 174–280. Plato manuscripts: *A Catalogue of Microfilms in the Plato Microfilm Project,* Yale University Library, ed. Robert S. Brumbaugh and Rulon Wells, 2 parts (New Haven, 1962). Tatakis, *La philosophie byzantine,*

tive kind appears in the eleventh century with Michael Psellos, a
man of considerable learning and influence.[27] He attempted a
kind of synthesis between Neoplatonic philosophy and Christian
theology that found many successors among the Byzantine
scholars of subsequent centuries. Following the precedent of
Proclus, Psellos included as a part of the Platonic tradition the
writings attributed to Hermes Trismegistus and the *Chaldaic Oracles.* The *Corpus Hermeticum,* as it has come down to us in Greek,
is perhaps an edition or anthology due to Psellos, and also the
collection of *Chaldaic Oracles* as we have it goes back to Psellos,
who added a commentary to it.[28] This commentary was known to
Ficino, who also translated part of Psellos' treatise *On demons,* and
to Francesco Patrizi, and it was printed in the sixteenth century.[29]

Among the Byzantine theologians we encounter a strong anti-
Platonist current, yet the detailed polemic against Plotinus and
Proclus, as we find it in the writings of Isaac Sebastocrator,
Nicolaus of Methone, and Nicephoros Chumnos, presupposes a
certain popularity of the Neoplatonic doctrines among their contemporaries. Chumnos' work against Plotinus was still copied in
the fifteenth century, although the name of the author was usually
distorted.[30] Nicolaus of Methone's critical notes on Proclus were

pp. 133–134. Pertusi, *Leonzio Pilato,* pp. 500–502. Krumbacher, *Geschichte
der byzantinischen Literatur,* p. 524. *Greek Manuscripts in the Bodleian
Library* (1966), p. 14–15, no. 5. M. Sicherl, "Platonismus und Textueber-
lieferung," *Jahrbuch der österreichischen byzantinischen Gesellschaft* 15
(1966), pp. 201–229.

27. Tatakis, *La philosophie byzantine,* pp. 161–210.

28. Hermès Trismégiste, ed. Nock and Festugière, Vol. 1 (Paris, 1945),
pp. xlix–li (where Psellos' editorship is discussed but doubted).

29. *Oracula magica Zoroastris cum scholiis Plethonis et Pselli,* ed. J.
Opsopoeus (Paris, 1599, first printed in 1589). For Ficino's translation, see
his *Opera,* II: 1939–1945.

30. Chumnos' *Antitheticum adversus Plotinum* was published in F.
Creuzer's edition of Plotinus, Vol. 2 (Oxford, 1835): 1413–1430, and in
Migne, *Patrologia Graeca,* Vol. 140, cols. 1404–1437. Cf. J. Verpeaux,
Nicéphore Choumnos (Paris, 1959), pp. 17–23, 141–146. Ševčenko,
Etudes sur la polémique entre Théodore Métochite et Nicéphore Choumnos

known to Ficino, and Ficino's manuscript of this work, with his Latin translation, has been rediscovered quite recently.[31] Finally, the writings of Isaac Sebastocrator against Proclus have been recently utilized to recover some important fragments of three lost theological works of Proclus that had been known up to that moment only through the Latin versions of William of Moerbeke.[32]

On the other hand, it would be quite wrong to assume that the Aristotelian tradition was lacking in strength among the Byzantines. The vast diffusion of Aristotle's writings among the Byzantines has been recently illustrated by a census of his Greek manuscripts.[33] There were important Byzantine commentators on Aristotle, such as Michael of Ephesus, Eustratius of Nicaea, and others,[34] and some of these Byzantine commentaries were translated into Latin during the Middle Ages or the Renaissance and

(Brussels, 1962). In late mss., the text usually appears under the name Kanikles or Charicles. Cf. V. Capocci, *Codices Barberiniani Graeci* 1 (Vatican City, 1958), p. 104, cod. 84.

31. M. Sicherl, "Neuentdeckte Handschriften von Marsilio Ficino und Johannes Reuchlin," *Scriptorium,* 16 (1962): 50–61 at 52 and 61. Cf. Nicolai Methonensis, *Refutatio institutionis theologicae Procli Platonici,* ed. J. Th. Voemel (Procli Diadochi et Olympiodori *in Platonis Alcibiadem Commentarii,* Vol. IV), Frankfurt, 1825.

32. *Procli Diadochi Tria Opuscula,* ed. H. Boese (Berlin, 1960). Isaak Sebastokrator, *Zehn Aporien ueber die Vorsehung,* ed. Johannes Dornseiff (Beitraege zur klassischen Philologie 19) [Meisenheim, 1966]. Isaak Sebastokrator's. . . . *De malorum subsistentia,* ed. James John Rizzo (Beitraege zur Klassischen Philologie 42) [Meisenheim, 1971].

33. A. Wartelle, *Inventaire des manuscrits grecs d'Aristote et de ses commentateurs* (Paris, 1963). A more detailed list is being prepared by Prof. Paul Moraux of the Free University, West Berlin. D. Harlfinger, *Die Textgeschichte der pseudo-aristotelischen Schrift, περὶ ἀτόμων γραμμάτων,* Amsterdam, 1971. K. Oehler, *Antike Philosophie und Byzantinisches Mittelalter* (Munich, 1969), 272–286.

34. The *Commentaria in Aristotelem Graeca* include the commentaries by Michael of Ephesus on the *Nicomachean Ethics* (Vol. 20) and on the *Parva Naturalia* (Vol. 22), those of Eustratius on the *Nicomachean Ethics* (Vol. 20) and on the *Analytica Posteriora* (Vol. 21). Also Stephanus' commentary on the *Rhetoric* (Vol. 21, pt. 2) and Sophonias' paraphrase of the *De anima* (Vol. 23) are Byzantine. For further commentaries, see Wartelle, *Inventaire des Manuscrits grecs d'Aristote et de ses commentateurs.*

thus exercised some influence on Western scholastic Aristotelianism.[35] Yet, Byzantine Aristotelianism, unlike its Arabic and Western counterparts, was never separated from the study of rhetoric or of the ancient poets and orators, and in most instances it was not even opposed to Platonism. If we consider the major Byzantine philosophers from Johannes Italos to the scholars of the fourteenth century, we encounter in most instances a combination of Aristotelian logic and physics with Platonist metaphysics, a combination that goes back to the ancient Neoplatonists and their Aristotelian commentaries.[36] It is often asserted that the philosophical and theological tradition of the Byzantine East was predominantly Aristotelian or anti-Platonist, but I have the impression that these statements are based to a large extent either on Western analogies or on certain polemical positions that appeared among the Byzantines only in the fifteenth century. I am inclined to think that the exclusive Aristotelianism of some Byzantine thinkers of the fourteenth and fifteenth centuries was due to Western influences which began to become important during that very period. Among the Latin authors translated into Greek at that time, we find not only Cicero and Ovid, Augustine and Boethius, but also Thomas Aquinas.[37]

It is against this background that we must understand the work of a thinker who was celebrated by his pupils and contemporaries as another Plato and who occupied in relation to the mature Platonism of the Western Renaissance a similar position as the last Byzantine philologists in relation to the Italian humanists:

35. For the medieval translation of Eustratius' and Michael of Ephesus' commentaries on the Nicomachean Ethics, see *Aristoteles Latinus, Codices,* Vol. 1 (Rome, 1939), p. 97.

36. Tatakis, *La philosophie byzantine,* pass. K. Krumbacher, *Geschichte der byzantinischen Literatur,* 2d ed. (Munich, 1897).

37. For the translations of Ovid, Cicero, Boethius, Augustine, and other Latin authors by Maximus Planudes, see Krumbacher, *Geschichte der byzantinischen Literatur,* p. 545. Cf. M. Rackl, "Die griechischen Augustinuebersetzungen," *Miscellanea Francesco Ehrle,* 1 (Studi e Testi 3, Rome, 1924): 1–38. For Aquinas, see below.

Georgios Gemistos Plethon.[38] He lived approximately from 1360 to 1452 and spent the greater part of his later life in Mistra, the capital of the despots of Morea, where he served as a counselor to the reigning princes and also gave instruction to some private pupils. He tried to strengthen the Byzantine Empire by a political reform based on ancient Greek models. According to the testimony of several contemporary enemies, which has been accepted by most recent scholars, Plethon also planned to restore the pagan religion of Greek antiquity. In the preserved fragments of his chief work, the *Laws,* he speaks at length of the ancient deities and their worship.[39] Yet, the work was destroyed after Plethon's death by his enemy Scholarios, who preserved only these paganizing passages in order to justify his action, and I suspect that the complete text of the work might have suggested an allegorical and less crude interpretation of the same passages. The part Plethon took in the Council of Florence, his theological opposition to the Union of the Greek and Latin Churches, and, finally, the unqualified admiration shown for Plethon by his pupil Cardinal Bessarion tend to cast some doubt on the supposed paganism of Plethon. On the other hand, Plethon always maintained a strict separation between his philosophy and Christian theology and never tried to harmonize them. In his extant writings he professes to be a convinced follower of Plato and his philosophy, and he often praises the Neoplatonic philosophers, especially Proclus by whom he was much influenced. He also likes to cite the early Oriental and Greek sages, especially the writings attributed to the Pythagoreans, and the so-called *Chaldaic Oracles,* which he apparently was the first to attribute to Zoroaster and on which he wrote a commentary.[40] His knowledge of the Orphic and Hermetic writings seems to be

38. See note 1 above.
39. Pléthon, *Traité des Lois,* ed. C. Alexandre and A. Pellissier (Paris, 1858, repr. Amsterdam, 1966).
40. On Plethon and the attribution of the oracles to Zoroaster, see J. Bidez and F. Cumont, *Les Mages hellénisés,* 2 vols. (Paris, 1938). For his commentary, see note 29 above.

established, although it appears less prominently in his writings, and the precedent of Proclus and Psellus would be sufficient to make such a knowledge plausible. Plethon cites the Stoics with favor but is strongly opposed to the Skeptics and especially to Aristotle. This anti-Aristotelianism is by no means typical of the Byzantine tradition; and since Plethon's famous treatise on the difference between Aristotle and Plato was composed during his stay in Italy and for his Italian friends,[41] I am inclined to interpret Plethon's anti-Aristotelianism as a reaction against the exclusive Aristotelianism which he encountered among the Latin theologians and which to him must have appeared excessive. Among the many characteristic points on which Plethon considers Plato to be superior to Aristotle, he insists on the reality of universals and ideas, on the divine origin of the world, and on the immortality of the soul. He also criticizes Aristotle's description of the moral virtues as means between two opposite vices, and he finally inisists that all events are due to necessary causes, defending also in his treatise *On fate* an extreme determinism that sounds more Stoic than Platonic.[42] We may note in Plethon's Platonism a strongly rationalistic character and the apparent absence of that mystical or spiritualistic element that is so prominent and central in the thought of the ancient Neoplatonists and of many Renaissance Platonists.

Plethon's treatise on the differences of Plato and Aristotle inaugurated the famous conroversy on the relative superiority of Plato and Aristotle that continued for several decades among the Byzantine and later among some Western scholars, a controversy that has been given an almost exaggerated importance in some

41. For Plethon's copy of the Orphic hymns, see R. and F. Masai, "L'oeuvre de Georges Gémiste Pléthon," *Académie Royale de Belgique, Bulletin de la Classe des Lettres,* ser. 5, Vol. 11 (1954): 536–555 at p. 546. For the complete text of Plethon's treatise on the differences between Plato and Aristotle, see Migne, *Patrologia Graeca,* Vol. 160, cols. 881–932. At the beginning, there is a characteristic attack on Averroes.

42. The *De fato* is a chapter (book II, ch. 6) from Plethon's *Laws.* It is printed in Alexandre and Pellissier, *Traité des Lois,* pp. 64–78.

historical accounts of the fifteenth century. However, the significance of this controversy should not be denied. If we disregard for the moment some discussions of special problems involved in the controversy, the first frontal attack against Plethon's treatise was composed by Scholarios around 1443.[43] It is a point by point defense of Aristotle against Plethon that shows a very detailed knowledge of the Aristotelian writings and emphasizes the agreement between Aristotelian philosophy and Christian theology. I am not inclined to attribute this exclusive and theological Aristotelianism of Scholarios to a supposed Byzantine theological tradition, as some historians have done, but rather to his obvious dependence on Western thought, and especially on Thomism. We know that Scholarios was more learned in Latin theology than in the Byzantine traditions of philosophy and philology, and his great admiration for Aquinas is documented by his numerous translations of his writings.[44] These facts are easily overlooked because in his later years Scholarios adopted a theological position hostile to the union with the Latin Church. This typically scholastic and Western attitude of Scholarios appears in the beginning pages of Scholarios' treatise, where he speaks with contempt of Plethon's Italian friends who are interested in Homer and Vergil, Cicero and Demosthenes and who hence admire Plato for his literary talent and are unable to judge the philosophical merit of Aristotle.[45] In this passage we find the typical Italian contrast between scholasticism and humanism translated into Greek. Plethon replied to Scholarios about 1449 in a treatise in which we note, among other things, the interesting remark that the basic agreement between

43. Georges Scholarios, *Oeuvres complètes,* ed. L. Petit, X. A. Siderides and M. Jugie, vol. 4 (Paris, 1935): 1–116.

44. Scholarios composed epitomes of Thomas' *Summa contra Gentiles* and of his *Summa Theologiae,* parts I and Ia IIae (*Oeuvres,* Vol. 5–6, 1931–1933). He also translated Thomas' commentary on Aristotle's *Physics,* books I–II, and his treatise *De fallaciis,* as well as Petrus Hispanus and Gilbertus Porretanus (*Oeuvres,* Vol. 8, 1936).

45. *Oeuvres,* 4:4.

Plato and Aristotle which Scholarios had attributed to the ancients appears only in Simplicius, who attempted to combine the doctrine of the two philosophers against that of the Christian Church.[46]

Aside from the controversy between Plethon and Scholarios, there was before and after the death of Plethon a discussion of more specific points of doctrine, such as the concept of substance or the doctrine of fate. In addition to Plethon and Bessarion, Theodore Gaza, Michael Apostolis, Andronicus Callistus, and several other Greek scholars participated in this discussion.[47] Most of their treatises were written in Italy but in the Greek language. They can now be read in recent editions, but no detailed history of the debate has yet been written, and I cannot enter into any further details. We must mention the treatise by George of Trebisond, *Comparationes philosophorum Platonis et Aristotelis,* which was written in Latin after Plethon's death, perhaps in 1455, and printed in the sixteenth century.[48] This work was much more violent than that of Scholarios in its doctrinal and personal attacks against Plethon and Plato himself, and it defended the superiority of Aristotle over Plato on all points, and especially his agreement with Christian theology. This attitude of Trapezuntius is rather strange when we consider his life and training.[49] He came at an early age from Crete to Italy, attended the school of Vittorino da Feltre in Mantua, and thus combined a Latin humanist education

46. Migne, *Patrologia Graeca,* Vol. 160, cols. 979–1020 at 981.
47. Cf. Mohler, *Kardinal Bessarion,* and Masai, *Pléthon et le Platonisme de Mistra.* For Gaza: A. Gercke, *Theodoros Gazes* (Greifswald, 1903). Theodore Gaza's *De fato,* ed. John Wilson Taylor, University of Toronto Studies, Philological Series, vol. 7 (Toronto, 1925). For Michael Apostolis: Deno J. Geanakoplos, *Greek Scholars in Venice* (Cambridge, Mass., 1962), pp. 73–110. For Andronicus Callistus: G. Cammelli, "Andronico Callisto," *La Rinascita,* 5 (1942): 104–121, 174–214.
48. Venice, 1523, repr. Frankfurt, 1965.
49. R. Sabbadini, "Briciole umanistiche V," *Giornale storico della letteratura italiana,* 18 (1891): 230–241; "Briciole umanistiche XXII," *ibid.,* 43 (1904): 253–254. G. Castellani, "Giorgio da Trebisonda maestro di eloquenza a Vicenza e a Venezia," *Nuovo Archivio Veneto,* 11 (1896): 123–142. A new monograph on Trapezuntius is being prepared by John Monfasani.

with his Byzantine background. He became a bilingual scholar, taught Greek in Venice for some time, made Latin translations from the Greek, especially of Aristotle, Ptolemy, Cyril, and Eusebius, but also of Plato's *Laws* and *Parmenides,* and composed letters and treatises in Latin, including influential handbooks of logic and of rhetoric.[50] His translations and treatises show a certain amount of interest in philosophy, to be sure, but his preparation was by no means theological or scholastic. Since he was involved in many controversies with other scholars, we might look for the motivation of his anti-Platonic treatise in his personal relations with Plethon's school. Perhaps he was also displeased with Plato's hostile attitude towards rhetoric and poetry, an attitude that for a humanist with a rhetorical training must have been difficult to swallow.

Trapezuntius' treatise provoked several answers, and it provided the occasion for Cardinal Bessarion to compose his great treatise *In calumniatorem Platonis.* This work, which was repeatedly revised by its author, was probably written between 1458 and 1469, first in Greek and then in a Latin version that was printed in 1469.[51] Bessarion not only defends Plato's life and doctrine against the attacks of Trapezuntius, but he also describes Plato's contributions to the various fields of learning and then presents Plato's metaphysical doctrines with an emphasis both on their intrinsic merits and on their agreement with Christian theology. Bessarion treats Aristotle with great respect and tends to harmonize him with Plato rather than to criticize him. He often cites the Latin theologians, especially Augustine, Aquinas, and Duns

---

50. For the translations of Plato, see R. Klibansky, "Plato's Parmenides in the Middle Ages and the Renaissance," *Medieval and Renaissance Studies,* 1 (1941–1943): 281–330 at 289–304. Garin, "Ricerche sulle traduzioni di Platone," pp. 372–373. For the translations of Aristotle, see E. Garin, "Le traduzioni umanistiche di Aristotele nel secolo XV," *Atti e Memorie dell' Accademia Fiorentina di Scienze' Morali "La Colombaria,"* 16 (N.S. 2, 1947): 55–104.

51. *Gesamtkatalog der Wiegendrucke* 4183. For the Greek and Latin text, see Mohler, *Kardinal Bessarion,* Vol. 2 (Paderborn, 1927).

Scotus. The general character of the work is apologetic rather than
philosophical, but it had the great merit of presenting to Latin
scholars for the first time a broad and balanced, although not
always accurate, picture of Plato's doctrine, based on a thorough
knowledge of his writings and of his ancient commentators. The
work had a wide circulation, being among the first books printed in
Italy,[52] and was enthusiastically received by several Greek, Italian, and French scholars whose letters have been preserved.[53]
Like Trapezuntius, Bessarion combined a Latin humanist culture
with a Byzantine training; and since he was a Cardinal of the
Roman Church, his published opinions were bound to carry great
weight and authority. Moreover, he was a patron of numerous
Greek and Italian scholars who were ready to defend and support
his work.

The famous controversy on Plato and Aristotle did not quite
end with Bessarion's work but continued for some time even after
its publication. Bessarion's influence may be felt not only in
Giovanni Andrea de' Bussi's preface to Apuleius[54] and in Perotti's
rebuttal of another lost work of Trapezuntius,[55] but also in a
series of treatises that are still unknown and unpublished by
Domizio Calderini, Fernando of Cordoba, and Andreas Con-
trarius. In another treatise that is still largely unpublished, Trapezuntius' son Andreas tries to defend his father's position against
Fernando of Cordoba.[56] To the sixteenth century already belongs
the unpublished treatise against Trapezuntius by the Augustinian

52. It was printed by Sweynheym and Pannartz, the two Germans who
introduced printing into Italy.
53. Bessarion's correspondence with Ficino, Argyropulus, Fichet, Perotti,
Omnibonus Leonicenus, Filelfo, Panormita and others is published in
Mohler, *Kardinal Bessarion,* Vol. 3 (Paderborn, 1942).
54. B. Botfield, *Prefaces to the First Editions of the Greek and Roman
Classics* (London, 1861), pp. 68–78.
55. Mohler, *Kardinal Bessarion,* 3: 343–375.
56. The beginning and end of Andreas Trapezuntius' treatise was published by F. A. Zaccaria, *Iter Litterarium per Italiam* (Venice, 1762), pp.
127–134. I hope to study and publish these treatises in collaboration with
John Monfasani and Frederick Purnell.

Hermit Ambrosius Flandinus,[57] a prolific author who also composed polemical treatises against Pomponazzi and Luther and voluminous commentaries on several works of Plato. We may find a last repercussion of the controversy, and even of Plethon's work, in the anti-Aristotelian polemic of an influential philosopher of the late sixteenth century who had received an excellent training in Greek and who spent a part of his life in Padua, in Venice, and in the Greek territories of Venice: Francesco Patrizi.[58]

In conclusion, I should like to discuss briefly the chief representatives of Western Platonism during the fifteenth century—Cusanus, Ficino, and Pico. They took no active part in the debate on Plato and Aristotle of which we have spoken, and a large part of their thought was either original, or may be traced to classical or medieval Western sources. Yet, we cannot conclude our discussion without mentioning the more or less obvious connections that link these Western Platonists with their Byzantine predecessors and contemporaries, and especially with Plethon and Bessarion.

It is not possible to reduce the thought of Cusanus, complex and original as it is, under the simple label of Platonism, but it is evident from his doctrines and quotations and from the content of his library that he was much attracted by Plato and his school.[59] The influence of Augustine and also that of the Areopagite and of Proclus on Cusanus' thought was decisive, and he stated explicitly that he discovered his doctrine of learned ignorance during his return from Constantinople. It now appears, however, that his knowledge of Greek was rather limited. We know little about his personal relations with Byzantine scholars except for his friendship with Bessarion, of which we have several testimonies, and the fact that other Byzantine scholars such as Athanasius of Constanti-

57. Paris, Bibliothèque Nationale, ms. lat. 6284.
58. *Discussiones Peripateticae* (Venice, 1571; enlarged edition, Basel, 1581).
59. E. Vansteenberghe, *Le cardinal Nicholas de Cues* (Paris, 1920, repr. Frankfurt, 1963). See note 62.

nople dedicated to him a few translations of Greek works into Latin.[60] Yet, Cusanus was surrounded by Italian humanists who were Greek scholars, especially Giannandrea de'Bussi, Bishop of Aleria, and Pietro Balbo, Bishop of Tropea, who belonged to his inner circle. We have learned rather recently that Plato's *Parmenides* and Proclus' *Platonic Theology* were translated for Cusanus, the former by Trapezuntius and the latter by Pietro Balbo,[61] and I discovered a Latin translation of Plethon's *De fato* by Johannes Sophianos that was made for Cusanus and apparently formed a part of his personal library.[62]

Whereas for Cusanus Platonism was an important part of his background, it constituted the very center of his work and thought for Marsilio Ficino. His Latin translation of Plato made the entire *Corpus* of Plato's dialogues available to Western readers for the first time, and hence it must be recorded as a major event in the history of Platonism and of Western thought. To this translation we must add his introductions and commentaries, among which the commentary on the *Symposium* was especially famous and influential; his translation and interpretation of Plotinus, which introduced this important thinker to the Western world, and his translations of various writings of other Neoplatonists such as Porphyry, Jamblichus, and Proclus, and of several pseudo-Platonic writers such as Hermes Trismegistus, Zoroaster, Orpheus, and Pythagoras. Ficino also presented Platonic philosophy, as he understood it, in his *Platonic Theology* and in his letters, and he

60. Vansteenberghe, pp. 29–30. For his return from Constantinople, see Cusanus, *De docta ignorantia,* ed. R. Klibansky (Leipzig, 1932), p. 163 (I was reminded of this passage by Prof. M. Watanabe).

61. Klibansky, see note 50 above. For the translation of Proclus' *Platonic Theology,* see R. Klibansky, *Proceedings of the British Academy* (1949), p. 11. H. D. Saffrey, "Sur la tradition manuscrite de la Théologie Platonicienne de Proclus," in *Autour d'Aristote, Recueil d'Etudes . . . offert à Monseigneur A. Mansion* (Louvain, 1955), pp. 387–430. P. O. Kristeller, *Iter Italicum,* Vol. 1 (London and Leyden, 1963): 8.

62. P. O. Kristeller, "A Latin Translation of Gemistos Plethon's *De fato* by Johannes Sophianos dedicated to Nicholas of Cusa," in *Nicolò Cusano agli Inizi del Mondo Moderno* (Florence, 1970), 175–193.

taught it in the courses and discussions of his Platonic Academy. We know from several statements in his writings that he considered the revival of Platonism as a task assigned to him by divine providence.[63]

If we ask what part, if any, Byzantine influences had in this revival of Platonism, we may give at least a partial answer to this question. Ficino himself states in the preface to his version of Plotinus (1492) that Cosimo de' Medici during the Council of Florence had heard some lectures by Plethon and was so deeply impressed by them that he conceived the idea of founding a Platonic Academy in Florence, a task for which he later chose Ficino when the latter was still young.[64] Knowing Ficino's manner of speaking, I hesitate to accept this story in as literal a sense as has been done by many historians, but there is a nucleus of truth in it, and Ficino surely intended to establish a historical link between his own work and that of Plethon. As a matter of fact, the passage is not completely isolated in the work of Ficino. He mentions Plethon in at least four other places, and one of them is of special interest since it says that Averroes misunderstood the thought of Aristotle because he did not know any Greek.[65] In an early preface of ten Platonic dialogues to Cosimo (1464), Ficino states that Plato's spirit flew from Byzantium to Florence.[66] We have recently learned that Ficino owned and partly copied in his own hand the Greek text of some of Plethon's writings.[67] I also found in

63. See note 1 above.
64. See note 24 above.
65. Kristeller, *Il pensiero,* p. 460. For the remark on Averroes, see *Opera,* p. 327.
66. *Supplementum Ficinianum,* ed. P. O. Kristeller, 2 (Florence, 1937): 104.
67. E. Garin, "Per la storia della cultura filosofica del Rinascimento," *Rivista critica di storia della filosofia,* 12 (1957): 3–21. Garin, "Platonici bizantini e platonici italiani," in his *Studi sul platonismo medievale* (Florence, 1958), pp. 153–219. A. Keller, "Two Byzantine Scholars and Their Reception in Italy," *Journal of the Warburg and Courtauld Institutes,* 20 (1957: 363–370. Cf. Kristeller, *Iter Italicum,* 1 (1963): 184.

a manuscript an anonymous Latin translation of Plethon's commentary on the *Chaldaic Oracles* and have some reason for attributing this translation to Ficino.[68] There are other traces of Byzantine influence in the work of Ficino. He copied with his own hand Traversari's translation of Aeneas of Gaza[69] and later translated a work of Psellos.[70] He corresponded with Bessarion and may have visited him, highly praised his work *In calumniatorem Platonis,* and included this work in a list of Platonist writings that he sent to his German friend Martin Brenninger.[71]

When we compare the works of Ficino with those of Plethon and Bessarion, however, we find few close similarities and a great discrepancy in their sources, problems, and intellectual interests. Ficino certainly agrees with Plethon in his historical conception that there was an ancient tradition of pagan theology that goes back beyond Plato to Pythagoras and the Chaldaeans, but Ficino may have derived this conception directly from Proclus rather than from Plethon. Yet, if it is true that Plethon was the first to attribute the *Chaldaic Oracles* to Zoroaster, Ficino would show in this matter his dependence on Plethon, for he often cites the *Oracles* with great respect and always treats them as the work of Zoroaster. Ficino's Platonism agrees with that of Plethon in the theory of ideas and in the doctrine of immortality, but I am inclined to think that these concepts are more central and more elaborate in Ficino than in Plethon. Ficino certainly rejects Plethon's fatalism, and since he emphasized the harmony between Platonic philosophy and Christian theology, he was far removed from the pagan tendencies attributed to Plethon. On this point, as well as in his comparatively tolerant attitude toward Aristotle, Ficino rather agreed with Bessarion. But unlike Bessarion, Ficino was not interested in attributing to Plato the specific doctrines of the

---

68. I hope to study this translation at a later date.
69. Kristeller, *Studies,* pp. 164–165.
70. See note 29 above.
71. *Opera,* p. 899.

various elementary and philosophical disciplines or of dogmatic theology. Vice versa, some of the fundamental teachings of Ficino's Platonism, such as the central position of man in the hierarchy of the universe, the spiritual experience of the contemplative life, or the doctrine of Platonic love, apparently did not occupy a significant place in the Platonism of his Byzantine predecessors.

If we pass from Ficino to Pico, the links with Byzantine Platonism become far less direct; for certainly Pico's scholastic training, which he received at Padua and Paris, his Averroism, and his enthusiasm for Hebrew theology and for the Cabala separate him much more decidedly than Ficino from the humanist tradition of Byzantine Platonism, and especially from Plethon.[72] But the famous project to establish a harmony between Plato and Aristotle as well as between their schools may be compared to a certain extent with the attitude of Bessarion.

When we proceed from the fifteenth to the sixteenth century, we notice some strongly anti-Aristotelian tendencies that come to a climax in the work of Francesco Patrizi and that may be connected more or less directly with the work of Plethon. Yet, the prevalent form in which the sixteenth century received the heritage of Platonism was that of Ficino and of Pico. The function of that

72. See notes 1 and 2 above. Francesco da Diacceto, Ficino's pupil and successor, wrote and probably lectured on both Plato and Aristotle. See Kristeller, *Studies,* pp. 287–336. For Francesco Patrizi, see note 58 above. In the sixteenth century a comparison between Plato and Aristotle was attempted, among others, by the following scholars: Bernardinus Donatus (*De Platonicae atque Aristotelicae philosophiae differentia,* printed with, and apparently based on, Plethon's treatise [Venice, 1540]); Sebastian Fox Morcillo (*De naturae philosophia seu de Platonis et Aristotelis consensione* [Louvain, 1554]); Jac. Carpentarius (*Platonis cum Aristotele in universa philosophia comparatio* [Paris, 1573]); Gabriel Buratellus (*Praecipuarum controversiarum Aristotelis et Platonis conciliatio* [Venice, 1573]); Jacopo Mazzoni (*De triplici hominum vita . . . methodi tres . . . in quibus omnes Platonis et Aristotelis . . . discordiae componuntur* [Cesena, 1576]; *In universam Platonis et Aristotelis philosophiam praeludia, sive de comparatione Platonis et Aristotelis* [Venice, 1597]). A study of this interesting topic is being prepared by Frederick Purnell. A Latin translation of Plethon's treatise by Nicolaus Scutellius (s. XVI) is found in Vienna, National-bibliothek, ms. 10056, f. 155–221v.

Platonism consisted in establishing a kind of rational metaphysics beside, rather than against, dogmatic theology and empirical science. The Platonist conceptions that were most popular in the sixteenth century were the doctrines of the contemplative life, of immortality, of the dignity of man, and of Platonic love. The historical conception of ancient theology found expression in the perennial philosophy of Augustinus Steuchus, which continued a notion derived from Proclus and Plethon and more directly from Ficino and Pico. Yet, Steuco's attempt to harmonize Platonism with Christian theology and even with Aristotelian science was closer to the attitude of Bessarion. It is the same attitude which we encounter in Raphael's Stanze, where the School of Athens is placed in front of the Disputation on the Sacrament and where Plato and Aristotle together occupy the center in a symbolic representation of secular philosophy.

Before concluding, I should like to correct a misunderstanding to which my position has sometimes given rise. I am convinced that the Platonism of the fifteenth century, as well as its humanism, were intellectual movements of great importance and some originality, but I never meant to give the impression that the intellectual life of the fifteenth century, or of the Renaissance in general, can be understood exclusively in terms of humanism and Platonism. There were also the powerful traditions of Aristotelian philosophy, of theology, of law, and of the various scientific disciplines, not to speak of the popular literature, the arts, and the religious, political, and economic life of the period. On the other hand, if we focus our attention on humanism and on Platonism alone, we notice in them a great variety of original and traditional elements. And among the traditional elements, great importance must be attributed to the influence of ancient and medieval Latin authors. I do not wish to deny any of these points even by implication. I have merely tried in this paper, according to its chosen topic, to emphasize the fact which I believe cannot be denied, that the Italian Platonism of the Renaissance, just as Renaissance humanism, received some important impulses from the Byzantine tradition. It was fortunate that Byzantine culture at the moment of its tragic end was able to transmit to the modern Western world the heritage of its thought, as well as of its scholarship and of its books, along with the ideas and texts which it had received from ancient Greece and which it had preserved for the future through a period of nearly a thousand years.

III Wimmer Lecture

6. Renaissance Philosophy and the Medieval Tradition

There are several good reasons why I begin this lecture with a genuine feeling of hesitation. It is a great honor to me, and also a great responsibility, to give a lecture in a series in which I have had many distinguished predecessors, one which is intended for publication and sponsored by a religious order noted throughout its long history for its devotion to learning and for its high standards of scholarship. Moreover, I am going to speak about a subject which is difficult and highly controversial, and to which I hardly can hope to do justice in a single lecture. Aside from the limitations of my own knowledge, of which I am fully aware, the state of scholarship in this area is such that nobody can hope to summarize it in a satisfactory way, whereas generalizations widely accepted in the past no longer seem to be sufficient. I am sure the task would have been easier fifty years ago, at least in appearance; and it might be easier fifty years hence. All I can hope to do in giving one hour or little more to a theme that would really require a lengthy book, is to give you a general impression based on my own studies (which are quite incomplete and uneven) and to rearrange some familiar facts in a different perspective. I shall try to supplement in this lecture what I said on another occasion about the classical influences in Renaissance thought.[1] Yet, I cannot completely avoid repeating a few things I have said or written elsewhere since I cannot change at will the historical facts, or my opinions about them, in the course of a few years.

Although I consider myself a realist in metaphysics, I am a thorough nominalist in reference to several terms employed in historical dicourse; therefore, I think it is necessary for me to define the meaning of the terms used in the title of this lecture. As you all know, the term Renaissance has been the topic of many debates and controversies and has been defined in a great variety of ways. As a result, the so-called problem of the Renaissance has become the subject matter of a whole literature.[2] I shall not attempt to enter into this debate today, but merely say that by Renaissance I mean roughly the period of Western European history between 1300 or 1350 and 1600. The controversies concerning the meaning of this period in Western history are partly due to national, religious, and professional ideals and preferences that have influenced the judgment of historians, and to the great complexity and diversity that belongs to the period itself and which will necessarily be reflected in the accounts of modern historians, depending upon those aspects which they choose to emphasize. The Renaissance includes many outstanding individuals who were very different from their contemporaries, but I do not think any individual ever can be said to speak for his age. There are great

1. *The Classics and Renaissance Thought,* Martin Classical Lectures delivered at Oberlin College (Cambridge, Mass., 1955). Reprinted with two additional papers under the title *Renaissance Thought* (New York, 1961).

2. See, among many other discussions, the symposium led by D. Durand and H. Baron and published in the *Journal of the History of Ideas,* 4 (1943): 1–74; *The Renaissance* (New York, 1953 and 1962); *The Renaissance,* ed. T. Helton (Madison, Wis., 1961); H. Weisinger, "Renaissance Accounts of the Revival of Learning," *Studies in Philology,* 44 (1948): 105–118. For a comprehensive history of the Renaissance concept, see W. K. Ferguson, *The Renaissance in Historical Thought* (Boston, 1948).

national, regional, and even local differences; and it will make a great difference in our account of the period on which countries or cities we focus our attention. Still it makes some sense to stress the predominant role of Italy and of the Low Countries during the Renaissance[3] and to acknowledge the fact that within the broader framework of European civilization, the cultural centers of gravitation lay in those parts, whereas in earlier or later periods it was located in France or in some other countries.

Moreover, within the larger Renaissance period that extends over several centuries there are different phases with distinct physiognomies; it is certainly true that the fourteenth century with Dante and even with Petrarch and Salutati was more medieval and less modern than the fifteenth with Bruni, Valla, and Alberti, or the sixteenth with Erasmus and Montaigne. Even within the same time and geographical area, different subjects and professions do not present a homogeneous picture. We do not find, and we cannot expect to find a parallel development in political and economic history, in theology, philosophy, and the sciences, in literature and the arts. In the Renaissance, just as in our own time or at any other time, we must be prepared to encounter a number of crosscurrents and conflicting currents even within the same place and time and subject matter. Certainly the spirit of the Renaissance to which some historians like to refer should be defined and demonstrated rather than merely asserted; and it would be wise to treat the unity of the period, not as an established fact, but rather as a regulative idea in the Kantian sense, something that may guide our investigations and that we hope to attain as a result of our studies, rather than as something we may take for granted at the beginning of our endeavors.

3. Two classical books on the fifteenth century, those of J. Burckhardt (*Die Cultur der Renaissance in Italian* [Basel, 1860, and many later editions]) and J. Huizinga (*The Waning of the Middle Ages,* tr. F. Hopman [London, 1924]), focus on Italy and the Low Countries respectively; and the considerable difference of their outlook derives to a large extent from this fact.

If my last statements may have sounded pleasing to the ears of medievalists, my next remark, I am afraid, will disappoint them. For what I have said about the Renaissance applies to an even larger degree to the Middle Ages, a much longer period of history generally taken to extend from 500 to 1300 or 1350. Although this is not frequently stressed, I cannot help noticing that the medieval period as a whole is as complex as the Renaissance, if not more so. Medieval culture is usually treated as a universal or international phenomenon, yet regional differences are by no means absent from it; the fact is merely concealed when a historian purporting to describe the history of the Middle Ages recounts in effect the medieval history of his own respective country.

Moreover, differences, for example, between the period of the barbaric invasions, the Carolingian age, and the twelfth or thirteenth century may seem even greater than those between the fourteenth and sixteenth centuries; and in the thirteenth century, after the rise of the universities, the specialization of learning and the diverse development of different sectors of civilization was as great, or nearly as great, as during the Renaissance.

In other words, a single medieval tradition does not exist; rather, there are many different medieval traditions, some of them quite opposed to others. We should really speak of medieval traditions, in the plural, or define in each instance which particular medieval tradition we have in mind. If it is true that the Renaissance in many of its aspects may be linked with medieval precedents, as I shall tend to confirm in this lecture, it is equally true that those medieval phenomena which seem to foreshadow certain Renaissance developments did not necessarily occupy the center of the stage during their own period, or especially during that phase of the Middle Ages that immediately preceded the early Renaissance.[4] Consequently, when we look for medieval precedents of

4. For example, classical humanism occupied a much more central position in the fifteenth century than did the *ars dictaminis* in the twelfth or thirteenth centuries, although the latter may be considered to some extent

the Renaissance, we may see the Middle Ages themselves in a different perspective from the one we usually have when we consider the medieval period in its own terms and with reference to its own prevailing trends. Such a different perspective may be instructive, as long as we do not pretend that it is the only legitimate one, just as it has been instructive to view classical antiquity occasionally in medieval or Renaissance perspective, as distinct from its own ancient perspective, or from what the nineteenth and twentieth centuries took that perspective to be.[5]

Further, I should say a few words about the term tradition, which has been a favorite with many scholars, including myself. Lately, historians have tended to stress continuity in history and to emphasize the fact that, even after a radical change such as a revolution or conquest, certain features of the previous order were retained. Yet, we should not forget that there are discontinuities in history and that even continuity means continuity in change, not merely pure stability. Stability is inertia, which belongs to things, to institutions rather than to human beings. Nor is any phase of human history so perfect that it would be worth preserving in all its aspects, even if that were possible. One of the most obvious causes for change, one that is usually forgotten by sociologists, is the fact that human beings are mortal and are inevitably replaced by new persons and new generations. In the long run, it is these new persons who will decide how much of what they receive from their predecessors will be preserved or changed, abandoned or destroyed. Traditions should be preserved whenever they represent genuine values (not all of them do). But in order to be kept alive, they must be appropriated by new generations; and thus they are

---

as the predecessor of the former. Moreover, those historians who stress the medieval antecedents of Renaissance humanism are apt to find them in the twelfth rather than in the thirteenth century.

5. This was done on a large scale by E. R. Curtius (*Europaeische Literatur und lateinisches Mittelalter* [Bern, 1948; Engl. trans., New York, 1953]). Cf. P. O. Kristeller, "Renaissanceforschung und Altertumswissenschaft," *Forschungen und Fortschritte,* 33 (1959): 363–369.

inevitably transformed. On the other hand, traditions may be effective, in a sense, even when they are not appropriated or continued, but reacted against.

When we ask what the medieval tradition, or the medieval traditions, meant in relation to the Renaissance, we must try to understand how many of these traditions the Renaissance retained and what it retained. The Renaissance retained some, perhaps many of the medieval traditions, but certainly not all. It made changes; and we must see these changes as well as the continuity. They may be subtle and hard to describe. Yet, in history, as in art and in life, nuances are as important as crude facts. And if they are hard to describe, the need for a penetrating study becomes the more imperative.

When I say the Renaissance made some changes, I do not mean only the original elements introduced by the Renaissance, or those elements in the Renaissance that seem to bring it closer to the modern age. I should like to include also the strengthening of classical influences which had been less effective during the Middle Ages; new approaches to familiar sources, for example, to the works of St. Augustine[6]; a new emphasis given to certain elements of the medieval tradition that had been present but less prominent during the Middle Ages; finally, a recombination and rearrangement of the very same older elements as they appear in a new and different looking whole.

Primarily the stability of traditions concerns general patterns such as literary and artistic genres, academic and professional methods and pursuits (although these too are subject to change), whereas within these general patterns there may be considerable changes and differences in style, quality, standing, and prestige,

6. For example, St. Augustine occupies a very important place in the work of Petrarch, but Petrarch's approach to St. Augustine is quite different from that of most medieval followers of St. Augustine. Cf. N. Iliescu, *Il canzoniere petrarchesco e Sant'Agostino* (Rome, 1962); P. O. Kristeller, *Studies in Renaissance Thought and Letters* (Rome, 1956), pp. 355–372; Kristeller, *Renaissance Thought* (1961), pp. 81–86.

and also in quantity. Some of the changes that occurred from the Middle Ages to the Renaissance may appear small from our modern perspective although they seemed important in their own time; this may be due to a foreshortening produced by our own distance from both periods. Obviously, the Renaissance must share with the Middle Ages the absence of all those elements of modern civilization that were the result of later developments. If the Renaissance lacks the physical science and philosophy of the seventeenth century, the technology, industrial economy, or political democracy of later periods, this does not make the Renaissance any more medieval than it would make the Middle Ages ancient or prehistoric.

Finally, I do not consider value judgments a part of the historian's task and should like to avoid them as much as possible. When a great medievalist once stated that the Renaissance is the Middle Ages minus God,[7] he pronounced an unfair value judgment in addition to committing a factual mistake. We must record past events as they are attested for us, whether we like them or not. We certainly cannot have it both ways and claim that the Renaissance was no different from the Middle Ages and also that it was inferior to them. Our likes and dislikes are unavoidable and hardly subject to discussion; but they are not relevant to our task as historians, nor will they undo those events which we happen to dislike. Moreover, we should admit that human "progress" has its limitations and that genuine progress is paid for by the loss of something else.

The last term which we should discuss is most difficult of all: philosophy. It is well known that every philosopher, depending on

7. E. Gilson, *Les idées et les lettres,* 2d ed. (Paris, 1955), p. 192: "La Renaissance, telle qu'on nous la décrit, n'est pas le moyen âge plus l'homme, mais le moyen âge moins Dieu . . ." I am aware of the qualification ("telle que l'on nous la décrit") and of the more perceptive remarks made by the same scholar elsewhere, especially in his paper, "Le moyen âge et le naturalisme antique," *Archives d'histoire doctrinale et littéraire du Moyen Age,* 7 (1932): 5–37.

his philosophy, has given a different definition of his subject. Moreover, philosophy is linked with many other aspects of human endeavor: religion and theology, law and politics, the sciences and scholarship, literature and the arts. These links are themselves subject to historical change. At the same time, philosophy has its own specific and professional tradition which distinguishes it from all those other pursuits with which it has been more or less intimately connected in various phases of its history. If we want to understand the role of philosophy in the Middle Ages and in the Renaissance, we must consider both aspects of philosophy, that is, its close links with other subjects, and its independent place within a broader and more complex system of thought and of culture.

In discussing our subject, I shall not attempt to consider individually the main schools and currents of Renaissance philosophy, describing for each of them its main ideas and its relations with medieval thought. Such a procedure would require much more time and space than I have at my disposal. I shall choose instead another procedure which may seem to be more ambitious and for which I may be less qualified. That is, I shall try to discuss briefly some of the main intellectual traditions of the Middle Ages and to ascertain what became of them during the Renaissance. In following this approach we shall view the Middle Ages in Renaissance perspective, but also the Renaissance in a medieval perspective. This does not mean that I wish to overlook or underestimate those aspects of Renaissance thought that were unrelated to the medieval tradition or that prepared the way for later, modern developments; but my very task will prompt me to place less explicit emphasis on them. I also fear that my all too broadly formulated topic will lead to an excessive amount of generalization and force me to reduce a great number of thoughts and thinkers to their least common denominator, for too broad a perspective makes everything look alike and appear almost empty. I hope to achieve a greater degree of concreteness by also paying some attention to specific currents and problems. Yet, the very attempt to compare large periods and broad traditions will force us to emphasize the general patterns which characterize them in their entirety and not those specific ideas which may be much more impressive, but which are distinctive of individual thinkers rather than of their school or period.

This survey must begin with the development of grammatical and rhetorical studies, since their development is closely linked, as we shall see, with the most pervasive intellectual movement of the Renaissance, humanism; also, during the Middle Ages they represent the earliest and most continuous tradition. Grammar and rhetoric were the main subjects of ancient Roman school instruction. The study of these subjects included the reading and interpretation of classical Latin poets and prose writers, as well as practical exercises in speech and writing.[8] Training in law was available to the future jurist or statesman, but there were no established schools of philosophy, medicine, or mathematics in the Western part of the Empire such as existed in the Greek East; this negative fact is important to remember since the Middle Ages were built upon a Roman and Latin, and not directly upon a Greek foundation.[9] The Christian Latin scholars of late antiquity who became the founders of the Middle Ages had absorbed the grammatical and rhetorical learning of the pagan schools. Some of them, such as Augustine and Boethius, were able to add to this background a thorough acquaintance with important sectors of Greek philosophy, known to them from extensive readings. Through their teaching and example, this heritage was bequeathed to subsequent centuries.[10]

During the early Middle Ages, learning became to a large extent

8. Charles S. Baldwin, *Ancient Rhetoric and Poetic* (New York, 1924); Donald L. Clark, *Rhetoric in Greco-Roman Education* (New York, 1957); H.-J. Marrou, *Histoire de l'éducation dans l'antiquité* (Paris, 1948).

9. H.-J. Marrou, *Saint Augustin et la fin de la culture classique* (Paris, 1938); P. Courcelle, *Les lettres grecques en Occident, De Macrobe à Cassiodore* (Paris, 1943); William H. Stahl, *Roman Science* (Madison, Wis., 1962).

10. E. K. Rand, *Founders of the Middle Ages* (Cambridge, Mass., 1928).

a monopoly of the clergy since the most important schools were those attached to the monasteries of the Benedictine order. Their instruction was based on the scheme of the so-called seven liberal arts which were considered the sum total of secular learning and identified with philosophy.[11] Within this cycle of subjects that included logic and the mathematical disciplines, grammar and rhetoric, and especially grammar, came to occupy the leading position. By then Latin had ceased to be the spoken language of Western Europe, but continued for many more centuries as the language of the Church and of learning, administration, and international diplomacy. Thus the study of the Latin language became the most elementary and also the most important part of grammatical instruction.[12] Yet, medieval grammatical studies at their best included also the reading and interpretation of the classical Latin authors and the composition of Latin prose and verse based on the imitation of these classical models.

The grammatical and rhetorical orientation of early medieval culture has become increasingly evident as the work of Irish and Carolingian scholars and the contribution of the cathedral schools down to the twelfth century has become better known. It appears in the form and content of the writings that have come down to us from the period, in the manuscripts of ancient authors which were copied and often glossed during this period, in the catalogues of its libraries, and in the testimonies about its schools. The rise of the universities and of scholasticism in the thirteenth century brought about a decline of grammatical and classical studies; but after the beginning of the fourteenth century, the tradition was resumed by

11. J. Mariétan, *Problème de la classification des sciences d'Aristote à St. Thomas* (Fribourg, 1901). M. Grabmann, *Geschichte der scholastischen Methode,* II (1957): 28–54; H.-J. Marrou, *Saint Augustin,* pp. 187 ff.; P. O. Kristeller, "The Modern System of the Arts," in *Renaissance Thought,* II (New York, 1965), pp. 163–227; *Artes Liberales,* ed. J. Koch (Leyden and Cologna, 1959); *Arts Libéraux et Philosophie au Moyen Age* (Montreal, 1969).

12. In the Italian vernacular of the thirteenth and fourteenth centuries, the word "grammatica" came to stand for the Latin language.

prehumanists and humanists of the early Italian Renaissance. The connection between French grammarians of the twelfth century and Italian humanists seems to be obvious, but the precise nature and extent of this connection has not yet been sufficiently explored. What is needed is a close analysis of the content and sources of the writings of the Italian prehumanists and humanists and especially of their commentaries on classical Latin authors. A comparison between these commentaries and those of the preceding centuries will no doubt go far in showing a certain continuity in the form and content of scholarship, and in the instruction through which this scholarship was transmitted.[13]

Yet, when the formal link between the grammatical studies of the Middle Ages and of Renaissance humanism has been recognized, their differences should not be overlooked. Although some of the formal pattern may seem to be the same, it remains to be seen how the quantity and quality of humanist learning compares with that of the medieval period. It is important to realize, as many students of the Renaissance have failed to do, that in one aspect of their activity Renaissance humanists were the professional successor of medieval grammarians. Yet, it is equally necessary to see, as many medievalists have refused to do, that in their knowledge of Latin and of the Latin classics Renaissance humanists made considerable advances over their medieval predecessors.

The difference between the classical learning of the humanists and that of the medieval grammarians becomes more marked when we pass from the study of Latin to that of Greek. The knowledge

13. F. Ghisalberti, "Giovanni del Virgilio espositore delle 'Metamorfosi,' " *Giornale Dantesco,* 34 (1933): 31 ff.; Eva M. Sanford, "The Manuscripts of Lucan," *Speculum,* 9 (1934): 278–295; Sanford, "Juvenal," in *Catalogus Translationum et Commentariorum,* Vol. I, ed. P. O. Kristeller (Washington, D.C., 1960): 175–238. Cf. P. O. Kristeller, *Renaissance Thought* (1961), p. 160. The prevailing view that classical studies declined in the thirteenth century has been qualified to some extent by E. K. Rand, "The Classics in the Thirteenth Century," *Speculum,* 4 (1929), pp. 249–269. See also H. Wieruszowski, "Rhetoric and the Classics in Italian Education of the Thirteenth Century," *Studia Gratiana,* 11, *Collectanea Stephan Kuttner,* I (Bologna, 1967): 169–207.

of Greek was not completely absent from the Middle Ages, as recent studies have convincingly shown; but it was never as common or as extensive as it was in Roman antiquity or during the Renaissance.[14] Many important texts were translated from Greek into Latin during the Middle Ages, and especially during the twelfth and thirteenth centuries. These translations played an important part in the study of Aristotelian philosophy and of the sciences, as we shall see.[15] Yet the Greek studies of Renaissance humanists went much further. They really mastered the language and its idioms; and their translating activity covered the entire range of ancient Greek literature, filling all the gaps that had been left by the medieval translators, and thus making many important authors and texts available to Western readers for the first time. The number and diffusion of humanist translations from the Greek is just now being more fully explored on the basis of the manuscript and printed sources.[16] Moreover, the humanists made new

14. L. R. Loomis, *Medieval Hellenism* (Lancaster, Pa., 1906); B. Bischoff, "Das griechische Element in der abendlaendischen Bildung des Mittelalters," *Byzantinische Zeitschrift,* 44 (1951): 27–55; K. M. Setton, "The Byzantine Background to the Italian Renaissance," *Proceedings of the American Philosophical Society,* 100 (1956): 1–76; R. Devreesse, *Les manuscrits grecs de l'Italie méridionale* (Studi e Testi 183, Vatican City, 1955); R. Weiss, "The Greek Culture of South Italy in the Later Middle Ages," *British Academy, Proceedings,* 37 (1951): 23–50; Weiss, "The Study of Greek in England during the Fourteenth Century," *Rinascimento,* II (1951): 209–239.

15. J. T. Muckle, "Greek Works Translated Directly into Latin before 1350," *Mediaeval Studies,* 4 (1942): 33–42; 5 (1943): 102–114. For translations from the Arabic and other languages, see M. Steinschneider, *Die europaeischen Uebersetzungen aus dem Arabischen bis Mitte des 17. Jahrhunderts* (Graz, 1956); G. Sarton, *Introduction to the History of Science,* 3 vols. (Baltimore, Md., 1927–1948).

16. *Catalogus Translationum et Commentariorum,* Vol. I, ed. P. O. Kristeller (Washington, D.C., 1960), especially for the article on Alexander of Aphrodisias by E. F. Cranz, pp. 77–135; Vol. II, ed. P. O. Kristeller and E. F. Cranz (1971), especially for the articles on St. Gregory Nazianzen by Sister Agnes Clare Way, pp. 43–192, and on Theophrastus by Charles B. Schmitt, pp. 239–322. See also R. J. Durling, "A Chronological Census of Renaissance Editions and Translations of Galen," *Journal of the Warburg and Courtauld Institutes,* 24 (1961), pp. 230–305; V. R. Giustiniani, "Sulle

translations of the same texts which had been translated before, for example, of Aristotle and of some of his commentators. It has been shown that in some instances the humanists merely revised some available medieval translations.[17] But, on the whole, we are not yet in a position to judge the relative merits of the medieval and humanist translations, say, of Aristotle, since to my knowledge nobody has yet taken the trouble to compare them with each other or with the Greek text. Under these circumstances, most of the judgments expressed by modern scholars on the subject must be considered gratuitous. There is no doubt that the Renaissance humanists were indebted for many aspects of their Greek learning to the Byzantine tradition; but this is a subject which has not yet been sufficiently studied, and it does not directly concern our topic.[18]

Rhetorical studies were in many ways connected with grammar; but, according to ancient tradition, they were considered more advanced. After the end of antiquity, the practice of public speech for which Roman rhetoric had been especially designed came to an end. Early medieval rhetoric was thus reduced to a theory of prose composition, and as such it occupied an important place in the curriculum. During the eleventh century at the latest, the eminently practical task of writing business letters and documents became

---

traduzioni latine delle 'Vite' di Plutarco nel Quattrocento," *Rinascimento* 12, N.S.I (1961): 3–62.

17. For Leonardo Bruni's translation of the Pseudo-Aristotelian *Oeconomica,* see H. Baron, *Humanistic and Political Literature in Florence and Venice at the Beginning of the Quattrocento* (Cambridge, Mass., 1955); J. Soudek, "The Genesis and Tradition of Leonardo Bruni's Annotated Latin Version of the (Pseudo-) Aristotelian 'Economics,'" *Scriptorium,* 12 (1958): 260–268; Soudek, "Leonardo Bruni and His Public: A Statistical and Interpretative Study of His Annotated Latin Version of the (Pseudo-) Aristotelian Economics," *Studies in Medieval and Renaissance History,* 5 (1968): 49–136.

18. K. M. Setton (see note 14 above); D. J. Geanakoplos, *Greek Scholars in Venice* (Cambridge, Mass., 1962); see also ch. 4 above. For a comparison between the medieval and humanistic translations of Aristotle, see P. O. Kristeller, *Studies in Renaissance Thought and Letters* (Rome, 1956), pp. 339 ff.

the subject matter of a special branch of rhetoric, called *dictamen,* which apparently originated in Montescassino and spread from there to the papal curia and the schools of Italy, France, and other countries.[19] The huge literature of *dictamen,* consisting of theoretical treatises and model collections, has been the subject of considerable study, especially the earlier period. Again, as in the case of commentaries on the Latin classics, there is a formal link between the medieval *dictamen* literature and the epistolography of the humanists. I have recently found and published a treatise on *dictamen* by one of the leading prehumanists, which seems to confirm this connection.[20] Yet, the persistence of a formal pattern should not prompt us to overlook the considerable differences in style and literary quality that separate the epistolography of the Renaissance humanists from that of their medieval predecessors. The Renaissance humanists were consummate classical scholars, as the medieval *dictatores* were not; and they shaped their letters, as far as possible, after classical models rather than after the business practice of the medieval chanceries.[21] The *dictamen* litera-

19. On medieval rhetoric in general, see Charles S. Baldwin, *Medieval Rhetoric and Poetic* (New York, 1928); R. McKeon, "Rhetoric in the Middle Ages," *Speculum,* 17 (1942): 1–32; For the *ars dictaminis,* see C. H. Haskins, *Studies in Medieval Culture* (Oxford, 1929). For further literature, see P. O. Kristeller, "Matteo de'Libri, Bolognese Notary of the Thirteenth Century, and his Artes Dictaminis," *Miscellanea Giovanni Galbiati,* II (Milan, 1951): 283–320; "Un'Ars Dictaminis di Giovanni del Virgilio," *Italia Medioevale e Umanistica,* 4 (1961): 181–200. To my knowledge, it has not been noticed that Gunzo of Novara (tenth century) in his well-known letter to the monks of Reichenau followed the scheme of the parts of a letter which was to be common in the theoretical treatises on Dictamen (Gunzo, *Epistola ad Augienses . . . ,* ed. K. Manitius [Weimar, 1958]). This scheme is based on the ancient doctrine of the parts of speech, to be sure. But it is a new thing to use the parts of speech as parts of the letter, adding the salutation which has no equivalent in the speech. Hence, it appears that the practice of letter writing preceded in this respect (and perhaps in other ways) the theory of the *dictamen,* and that the origin of such characteristic theories as the six parts of the letter must be traced back beyond the earliest extant writers on *dictamen.*

20. See note 19.

21. For a characteristic discussion of this question, see P. O. Kristeller, "An Unknown Correspondence of Alessandro Braccesi with Niccolò

ture deserves considerable respect and attention for its great practical and cultural importance, but any reader imbued with a moderate amount of classical training can hardly help finding the letters of the humanists more interesting and more enjoyable.

I should like to insist that the core of the medieval rhetorical tradition lies in the *dictamen,* and not in the study of Aristotle's *Rhetoric,* which has received much greater attention from some recent historians of the subject.[22] Aristotle's *Rhetoric* was studied in the thirteenth and fourteenth centuries by Aristotelian philosophers, rather than by the professional rhetoricians, and for good reasons in close connection with Aristotle's writings on moral philosophy.[23] Yet, this is a narrow trickle compared with the broad stream of the *dictamen* which leads gradually but directly into the equally broad current of humanist rhetoric and epistolography. It is true that the *dictamen* had no connection with Aristotelian philosophy and that its philosophical content is meager; but it is historically significant that the *dictatores* in their prologues made at least some philosophical claims and pretensions for their discipline.[24] This claim, empty as it may appear to us, links the *dictatores* not

---

Michelozzi, Naldo Naldi, Bartolommeo Scala, and other Humanists (1470–1472) in Ms. Bodl. Auct. F.2.17," in *Classical Medieval and Renaissance Studies in honor of Berthold Louis Ullman,* II (Rome, 1964), pp. 311–363.

22. R. McKeon ("Rhetoric in the Middle Ages," see note 19 above), hardly mentions the *dictamen.*

23. This is quite evident from the manuscripts containing the *Rhetoric* and described in the *Aristoteles Latinus, Codices,* 3 vols., ed. G. Lacombe and others (Rome, 1939– Bruges and Paris, 1961). Commentaries on Aristotle's *Rhetoric* were composed by such scholastic philosophers as Aegidius Romanus, Guido Vernanus of Rimini, and Johannes de Janduno but not by any of the professional rhetoricians or *dictatores* prior to the fifteenth century. In the Greek manuscript tradition, the *Rhetoric* does not appear among the ethical works of Aristotle. See A. Wartelle, *Inventaire des Manuscrits Grecs d'Aristote et de ses commentateurs* (Paris, 1963).

24. Several *dictatores* claim philosophical importance for their subject in their prefaces. Cf. H. Wieruszowski, "Ars Dictaminis in the Time of Dante," *Medievalia et Humanistica,* I (1943): 95–108 at p. 105.

only with the early medieval tradition of the *Artes Liberales,* but also with the program of ancient and Renaissance rhetoric.

The practice of public speaking that disappeared at the end of antiquity, along with political and legal institutions on which it depended, came to be revived in late medieval Italy with the rise of city republics and the revival of Roman law during the thirteenth century, if not earlier.[25] It was soon made the subject of theoretical and practical instruction. The treatises on the *ars arengandi* and the surviving model speeches cannot compare in number or diffusion with the vast literature on *dictamen,* but their very existence is sufficient to prove the rise and relative importance of secular oratory as a historical phenomenon which until very recently had been overlooked by most students of medieval rhetoric. The study of this material is still in its early stage, but it can be shown easily that all major types of Renaissance oratory made their first appearance in late medieval Italy and that there is a close and direct formal connection between medieval and humanist oratory. And again we must add that humanist orations are very different from their medieval counterparts and, in my opinion, superior to them in style and learning, if not in historical interest.

The rise of humanistic studies in the Renaissance was not a phenomenon restricted to the area of grammatical and rhetorical studies, as some of my previous remarks might have suggested, but it had a tremendous impact upon all other areas of learning and civilization, including philosophy. Practically all sources of Greek philosophy became known either for the first time or through new and reputedly better translations. Many medievalists fail to appreciate this development or to realize that the sources of ancient

25. Kristeller, *Renaissance Thought* (1961), pp. 104–105, 158–159. A. Galletti, *L'Eloquenza* (Milan, 1904–1938). For humanist rhetoric see Charles S. Baldwin, *Renaissance Literary Theory and Practice* (New York, 1939); Donald L. Clark, *Rhetoric and Poetry in the Renaissance* (New York, 1922); O. B. Hardison, *The Enduring Monument* (Chapel Hill, N.C., 1962).

thought available to medieval thinkers were quite limited and indirect compared with the actual body of extant Greek literature, although the twelfth and thirteenth centuries exhibited great activity in translation. In the wake of Renaissance humanism, ancient philosophies other than Aristotelianism became much better known and were revived: philosophies such as Stoicism, Epicureanism, and Skepticism, not to speak of Platonism which occupied a place of its own and of which we shall have more to say later on.

Under the influence of their rhetorical and cultural ideals, the humanists brought about a thorough change not only in the sources, but also in the style, terminology, and literary genres of philosophical writing. They coined (after ancient precedents) the term *studia humanitatis* (humanities) for their studies[26] and formulated a new educational and cultural ideal that went a long way to enhance their prestige and influence.[27] They also claimed to accomplish a rebirth of learning and letters and thus were responsible for the name "Renaissance" by which the entire period is known to us.[28]

In making these claims, the humanists were no doubt unfair to their medieval predecessors; but they were trying to assert the importance of their field, the humanities, against the traditional claims of other subjects. This is the meaning of the so-called defense of poetry on the part of early humanists (where poetry stands for humanist learning) and of their repeated attacks on scholasticism.

26. A. Campana, "The Origin of the Word 'Humanist,'" *Journal of the Warburg and Courtauld Institutes,* 9 (1946): 60–73; Kristeller, *Renaissance Thought,* pp. 110–111; G. Billanovich, "Da autorista ad umanista," in *Wort und Text, Festschrift fuer Fritz Schalk* (Frankfurt, 1963), pp. 161–166.
27. W. H. Woodward, *Studies in Education during the Age of the Renaissance* (Cambridge, 1906); E. Garin, *Il pensiero pedagogico dello umanesimo* (Florence, 1958).
28. W. K. Ferguson, *The Renaissance in Historical Thought;* H. Weisinger, "Renaissance Accounts of the Revival of Learning," *Studies in Philology,* 45 (1948): 105–118.

The humanists were engaged in transforming the entire system of secondary education and in imposing their scholarly and stylistic standards upon the other academic disciplines, and to some extent they succeeded. They did not, however, replace the traditional subject matter of these disciplines, although one of their latest and most brilliant representatives, the Spaniard Vives, also attempted to accomplish that.

As far as philosophy is concerned, the humanists considered moral thought their province. They produced a large literature of moral treatises, dialogues, and essays. The moral ideas of Petrarch and Alberti, of Erasmus and Montaigne, and many other scholars constitute the most direct contribution of Renaissance humanism to the history of Western thought.

Leaving aside a number of important specific ideas which are the property of individual humanists rather than of the entire movement, the main contribution of Renaissance humanism seems to lie in the tremendous expansion of secular culture and learning which it brought about in the areas of literature, historiography, and moral thought. This development was not entirely new and to some extent may be traced back to the later Middle Ages; but it did reach its climax during the Renaissance.

There is some justification in the statement that the humanist program and contribution was in its core cultural rather than philosophical. It omitted several problems and areas that form an integral part of philosophy as previously or commonly understood, and it included many subjects such as literature and historical scholarship that are usually not considered a part of philosophy. Yet, in our time, when many people take the praise of the sciences as a substitute for philosophy, we might forgive the humanists for having done the same with the humanities. And, after all, there are philosophical problems and implications in the humanities as there are in the sciences.

The concern of Renaissance humanists with the classics and secular learning led many contemporary critics and modern his-

torians to label them as pagan, but this charge can hardly be
sustained in the light of our present information. If we call Alberti
pagan for not referring to Christian sources in his moral writings,
we should have to say the same about Boethius. It is fashionable
now in certain popular circles to maintain that our entire spiritual
and moral heritage is due to what is called the "Judaeo-Christian"
tradition. Such a claim reveals an abysmal ignorance of the real
history of Western thought. For the roots of many of our basic
ideas lie in Greek philosophy; these ideas have never ceased to
exert a direct influence and have been themselves assimilated in
various ways into the Jewish and Christian traditions.[29]

It is now time for us to say a few words about the medieval
tradition of Christian theology and about its transformation during
the Renaissance. The origin and rise of the Christian religion, the
development of its main theological doctrines, and its synthesis
with the literary and philosophical traditions of the Greeks and
Romans still belong to the later phases of classical antiquity. This
process was almost completed before the beginning of the Middle
Ages. Christianity and Catholicism are no more medieval than
they are ancient or modern. Whereas nobody would deny that
religion and theology played a dominating role in the Middle Ages,
it has become increasingly clear that medieval thought and learning were never completely limited to theology. Even in the early
Middle Ages grammar and the other liberal arts were studied apart
from theology, though usually as a preparation for it. During the

29. S. Lieberman, *Greek in Jewish Palestine* (New York, 1942); Lieberman, *Hellenism in Jewish Palestine* (New York, 1950); F. C. Grant,
Roman Hellenism and the New Testament (New York, 1962); E. Hatch,
The Influence of Greek Ideas on Christianity, ed. F. C. Grant (New York,
1957). Ch. N. Cochrane (*Christianity and Classical Culture* [London,
1944]) credits the Church fathers and even St. Augustine with philosophical
originality on many points where they actually depend on Stoic or
Neoplatonic sources (see my review in *The Journal of Philosophy,* 41
[1944]: 576–581). The literature on the classical influences on the Church
fathers is far too large to be cited in detail.

high Middle Ages theology itself underwent important changes.[30] In the eleventh and twelfth centuries, the study of logic and dialectic began to expand at the expense of grammar and rhetoric, especially in the schools of Northern France; the forms of the question and of the commentary became more fully developed; and the new method of logical argument was applied to the subject matter of theology. This is the precise meaning of the term "scholastic theology"; and the attitude of John of Salisbury or of St. Bernard of Clairvaux shows that its rise met with resistance even among scholars of unquestioned intellectual and religious integrity.

Another change that accompanied this development was the effort to transform Christian doctrine from scattered pronouncements of Scripture, the Councils, and the Church Fathers into a coherent and systematic body of statements. This process culminates in Peter Lombard's *Sentences,* the leading theological textbook of the subsequent centuries, and in St. Thomas Aquinas' *Summa Theologiae.*

During the thirteenth and fourteenth centuries, theology came to be taught at Paris and other universities alongside with other learned disciplines; it tended to abandon its previous reliance on the writings of St. Augustine and to ally itself to an increasing degree with Aristotelian philosophy. St. Albertus Magnus, St. Thomas Aquinas, Johannes Duns Scotus, William of Ockam, and the Averroist Siger of Brabant represent different types and phases of this Aristotelianizing theology.

When we pass from the late Middle Ages into the Renaissance, we note that the traditions of scholastic or Aristotelian theology were vigorously continued. The theological schools of Thomism, Scotism, and Ockamism all had numerous followers. It can be

30. M. Grabmann, *Die Geschichte der katholischen Theologie* (Freiburg, 1933; repr. Darmstadt, 1961); A. M. Landgraf, *Einfuehrung in die Geschichte der theologischen Literatur der Fruehscholastik* (Regensburg, 1948); J. de Ghellinck, *Le mouvement théologique du XII e siècle,* 2d ed. (Brussels and Paris, 1948).

shown that during that period Thomism began to exert a much greater influence outside the Dominican order than during the thirteenth or fourteenth century.[31] It has been shown that Luther's theology was influenced by the strong Ockamism of the German universities of the fifteenth century,[32] and it has now become fashionable to call him a medieval thinker. On the other hand, Catholic theology experienced a strong revival during the sixteenth century after the founding of the Jesuit order and the Council of Trent, especially at the Universities of Spain and Portugal; and this revival is linked in many ways with the ideas and methods of St. Thomas and other medieval theologians.[33]

It would be a mistake, however, to overlook the impact of the humanist movement upon Renaissance theology. Those humanists who were explicitly concerned with theological questions (and we might as well call them Christian humanists) were by no means opposed to religion or theology as such, but they criticized scholastic theology in the name of simple piety and religious scholarship in accordance with their own ideals. They preferred St. Bernard to the scholastics, considered the Church Fathers as the Christian classics, insisted that they were grammarians rather than dialecticians in the medieval sense, and advocated the direct study of Scripture. They also proceeded to apply their new methods of philological and historical scholarship to the textual study and interpretation of Scripture and early Church writers.[34]

31. F. Ehrle, *Der Sentenzenkommentar Peters von Candia* (Münster, 1925); R. Garcia Villoslada, *La Universidad de Paris durante los estudios de Francisco de Vitoria* (Rome, 1938).

32. R. H. Bainton, *Here I Stand: A Life of Martin Luther* (New York, 1950); H. A. Oberman, *The Harvest of Medieval Theology* (Cambridge, Mass., 1963).

33. M. Grabmann, *Die Geschichte der katholischen Theologie* (Freiburg, 1933); C. Giacon, *La seconda scolastica*, 3 vols. (Milan, 1944–1950); F. Copleston, *A History of Philosophy*, Vol. III (Westminster, 1953).

34. Kristeller, *Renaissance Thought*, ch. 4; E. H. Harbison, *The Christian Scholar in the Age of the Reformation* (New York, 1956); P. Polman, *L'élément historique dans la controverse religieuse du XVI e siècle*

This humanist approach to theology may be traced from Petrarch to Erasmus, and it left a powerful impact upon Catholics and Protestants alike. Even Luther is not untouched by it, whereas it is easy to discern its influence in Melanchthon and Calvin as well as in some of the Spanish theologians.

The Renaissance may have produced some scholars and thinkers who were indifferent to Christianity or estranged from some of its teachings. But as a whole, the period is far from being un-Christian as it has sometimes been represented. Certainly the term Christian philosophy, which has recently been used to characterize medieval thought,[35] would have been more easily understood by some of the Renaissance humanists than by the medieval scholastics. It is Erasmus who speaks of the Philosophy of Christ, as Justinus Martyr had done in the second century.[36] Thomas Aquinas could not and did not use this phrase. For him theology was Christian, to be sure, but philosophy was Aristotelian; and the question was not to substitute Christian for Aristotelian philos-

---

(Gembloux, 1932); A. Hyma, *The Christian Renaissance* (New York, 1924).

35. Especially by E. Gilson (*L'esprit de la philosophie médiévale*, 2d ed. [Paris, 1944]; *History of Christian Philosophy in the Middle Ages* [New York, 1955]). I do not deny, of course, that the medieval philosophers were Christians and that their philosophy, for this and other reasons, must be distinguished from that of their Islamic and Jewish contemporaries. Yet to my knowledge the term "Christian philosophy" is not used by any of the medieval thinkers whom Gilson has in mind, and this fact seems to me significant.

36. Erasmus uses the terms *philosophia Christi* and *philosophia Christiana* repeatedly, especially in the prefaces of his *Enchiridion* and of his edition of the *New Testament* (*Ausgewaehlte Werke*, ed. A. M. and H. Holborn [Munich, 1933], pp. 5–7, 9, 139ff.). For Justinus Martyr, the crucial passage is found in the *Dialogus cum Tryphone*, ch. 8, Vol. I, ed. G. Archambault, (Paris, 1909), p. 40: διαλεγόμενός τε πρὸς ἐμαυτὸν τοὺς λόγους αὐτοῦ ταύτην μόνην εὕρισκον φιλοσοφίαν ἀσφαλῆ τε καὶ σύμφορον. οὕτως δὴ καὶ διὰ ταῦτα φιλόσοφος ἐγώ. For the idea in Justin and other early Apologists, see M. V. Engelhardt, *Das Christenthum Justins des Maertyrers* (Erlangen, 1878), pp. 223–231; C. Clemen, *Die religionsphilosophische Bedeutung des stoisch-christlichen Eudaemonismus in Justins Apologie* (Leipzig, 1890); J. Quasten, *Patrology*, Vol. I (Utrecht, 1950), pp. 196 and 220.

ophy, but to determine their relationship and to reconcile them as far as possible.

This problem of the relationship between philosophy and theology continued to preoccupy the thinkers of the Renaissance as it had worried Thomas Aquinas and the other scholastics. The very existence of the problem shows that, contrary to frequent modern claims, philosophy in the thirteenth century, if not before, was distinct from theology, though subordinate and not opposed to it. In the fourteenth century, even at Paris, the teaching of philosophy was more and more divorced from theology; and the prevailing tendency among philosophers was to recognize the basic superiority of theology, but to assert at the same time the relative independence of philosophy within its own domain. It is the position which Siger of Brabant took, and it is usually referred to as "Averroism" or as "the doctrine of the double truth."[37]

The Italian Aristotelians of the Renaissance, such as Pomponazzi, inherited this position from their medieval predecessors.[38] On the other hand, Renaissance Platonists emphasized the harmony between religion and philosophy and thus came closer to the position of St. Thomas, although they tended to grant philosophy more equality and independence than medieval theologians would have done.[39] This is a nice example of the inadequacy of labels usually employed in historical discourse about these subjects and of the fact that there are several medieval traditions and several Renaissance philosophies. Each Renaissance philosophy has different medieval sources and antecedents; and even if we succeed in establishing the right connections, the presence of a link

37. E. Renan, *Averroès et l'averroïsme* (Paris, 1852); P. Mandonnet, *Siger de Brabant et l'averroïsme latin au XIII e siècle*, 2d ed. (Louvain, 1908–1911); S. MacClintock, *Perversity and Error: Studies on the "Averroist" John of Jandun* (Bloomington, Ind., 1956).

38. B. Nardi, *Sigieri di Brabante nel pensiero del Rinascimento italiano* (Rome, 1945); Nardi, *Saggi sull'Aristotelismo Padovano dal secolo XIV al XVI* (Florence, 1958).

39. P. O. Kristeller, *Il pensiero filosofico di Marsilio Ficino* (Florence, 1953), pp. 18–20; 346–349.

does not mean that a given system of thought occupied the same place within its own time as its predecessor had done within the previous period.

We can touch but briefly upon another branch of learning which had great importance both during the Middle Ages and the Renaissance, but which for a variety of reasons had but tenuous connections with the mainstream of philosophical thought during those periods: jurisprudence. In the earlier Middle Ages, study of both civil and canon law was somewhat submerged and seems to have been largely carried on within the broader framework of the seven liberal arts. After the eleventh century, the study of canon law underwent a development similar to theology: it was subjected to the new methods of dialectic, and it received a systematic order and arrangement in Gratian's *Decretum* and other great canonist collections.[40]

In the case of civil law the main fact, aside from dialectical method, was the adoption of the Roman *Corpus Iuris* as the authoritative textbook of instruction at Bologna and other law schools and its reception as a valid law code in Italy and elsewhere.[41]

When we pass from the Middle Ages to the Renaissance, we note an unbroken continuity of legal teaching as well as a voluminous body of legal commentaries, questions, and opinions (*consilia*) which for the later period have been hardly sorted, let alone studied, and are sometimes treated by historians as if they did not exist.

Aside from this legal tradition, often referred to as *Mos Italicus,* because it was most strongly represented at the Italian law schools,

40. J. F. von Schulte, *Die Geschichte der Quellen und Literatur des canonischen Rechts,* 3 vols. (Stuttgart, 1875–1880); S. Kuttner, *Repertorium der Kanonistik,* Vol. I (Vatican City, 1937); J. de Ghellinck, *Le mouvement théologique au XII e siècle,* 2d ed. (Brussels and Paris, 1948).
41. F. K. von Savigny, *Geschichte des roemischen Rechts im Mittelalter,* 2d ed., 7 vols. (Heidelberg, 1834–1851); H. Kantorowicz, *Studies in the Glossators of the Roman Law* (Cambridge, 1938).

Renaissance humanism had a strong impact on jurisprudence, which culminated in the sixteenth century under the name of *Mos Gallicus*. Its main tendency was to replace the abstract dialectical method of the medieval jurists with a philological and historical interpretation of the sources of Roman law. If the ties between legal practice and the Roman law were reportedly weakened as a result of this development, historical understanding of the Roman law certainly made tremendous progress.[42]

The philosophical significance of the legal tradition lies primarily in the area of political thought; and it is significant that some of the leading political thinkers of the sixteenth century, such as Jean Bodin, had received legal training.[43] We may add the concept of natural law, in important notion which originated in Stoic philosophy and was introduced from Stoic sources into the very text of the Roman law.[44] When adopted by St. Augustine, it was reinterpreted in a Neoplatonic fashion[45] and bequeathed in this form to Thomas Aquinas and other medieval theologians. The revival of this doctrine in the seventeenth century owes much to the legal and theological thought of the sixteenth century. It is now fashionable to consider the doctrine of natural law as antiquated, but I do not see how we can ever subject a given positive law to moral criticism unless we maintain a universally valid moral standard by which it may be judged and measured.

42. G. Kisch, *Humanismus und Jurisprudenz* (Basel, 1955); the same, *Erasmus und die Jurisprudenz seiner Zeit* (Basel, 1960); D. Maffei, *Gli inizi dell'umanesimo giuridico* (Milan, 1956).

43. P. Mesnard, *L'essor de la philosophie politique au XVI e siècle* (Paris, 1936, repr. 1951).

44. The beginning sentence of Chrysippus' treatise on law has been preserved because it was inserted verbatim in the *Corpus Iuris* (Dig., I, 3, 2, citing "Marcianus libro primo institutionum"). Cf. H. von Arnim, *Stoicorum Veterum Fragmenta*, Vol. III (Leipzig, 1903), p. 77, no. 314 (who mentions Marcianus, but not the *Corpus Iuris*).

45. *De ordine*, II, 8, 25. *De vera religione*, 31, 58. *De libero arbitrio*, I, 6. Cf. E. Gilson, *Introduction à l'étude de Saint Augustin*, 3d ed. (Paris, 1949), p. 168. St. Thomas Aquinas, *Summa Theologiae*, I–II ae, qu. 91–95. Cf. also Gratian, *Decretum*, Dist. I, C.7.

The scientific traditions of the Middle Ages which we must mention, at least in passing, have been the subject of many recent studies; they have also played a central role in the often heated controversies about the relation between the Middle Ages and the Renaissance, and about the merits and contributions of these two periods.[46] I should like to stress that in my opinion there is no such thing as Science with a capital S, but that there is a variety of different sciences, each with its own tradition and historical development. Only two sciences, or groups of sciences, had from antiquity a separate history that was relatively, if not entirely, independent of philosophy: medicine, and the mathematical disciplines including astronomy.

The early Middle Ages inherited but a small share of the rich heritage of ancient Greek medicine. Medical theory was usually treated as an appendix to the seven liberal arts, and medical practice was often exercised by people without learning or formal theoretical training.[47] The main changes occurred again during the twelfth century. A sizable body of more or less advanced medical treatises were translated from Greek and Arabic and adopted as textbooks for medical instruction. At the same time, medical theory underwent the influence of scholastic logic and found its literary expression in commentaries and questions. The school of Salerno, which in an earlier period had originated as a society of

46. P. Duhem, *Etudes sur Léonard de Vinci*, 3 vols. (Paris, 1906–1913); E. Moody, "Galileo and Avempace," *Journal of the History of Ideas*, 12 (1951): 163–193, 375–422; M. Clagett, *Giovanni Marliani and Late Medieval Physics* (New York, 1941); Clagett, *The Science of Mechanics in the Middle Ages* (Madison, Wis., 1959); A. Maier, *Die Vorlaeufer Galileis im 14. Jahrhundert* (Rome, 1949); Maier, *An der Grenze von Scholastik und Naturwissenschaft*, 2d ed. (Rome, 1952); *Zwischen Philosophie und Mechanik* (Rome, 1958); A. C. Crombie, *Augustine to Galileo* (London, 1952); E. Rosen, "Renaissance Science As Seen by Burckhardt and His Successors," in *The Renaissance*, ed. T. Helton (Madison, Wis., 1961), pp. 77–103.

47. L. C. MacKinney, *Early Medieval Medicine* (Baltimore, Md., 1937); H. E. Sigerist, "The Latin Medical Literature of the Early Middle Ages," *Journal of the History of Medicine*, 13 (1958): 127–146; A. Beccaria, *I codici di medicina del periodo presalernitano* (Rome, 1956).

practitioners, shows this transformation in the direction of theory and scholasticism during the course of the twelfth century; and the same is true of Montpellier and the other centers of medical study. At the same time, medicine formed an alliance with Aristotelian philosophy which was to remain characteristic of the Italian universities far into the Renaissance.[48] This alliance accounts, at least in part, for the secular and "Averroistic" character of Italian Aristotelianism, which has been noted by many historians.

In spite of this continuity, Renaissance medicine underwent the influence of humanism no less than did theology or law. Several writings of Hippocrates and Galen were widely known since the twelfth century or even earlier, others since the fourteenth century, but a surprisingly large number of their works were translated for the first time between the fifteenth and sixteenth centuries.[49] The significance of this fact will become fully apparent when the contribution of these newly translated ancient writings to medical knowledge are carefully studied and evaluated, something which to my knowledge has not yet been done.

On the other hand, a subject such as anatomy or surgery, which benefited less from theory than from observation and practice, made steady progress during the sixteenth century. A figure such as Paracelsus illustrates that a real or imagined emancipation from ancient authorities could attain at least a certain measure of success.

Of even greater historical significance was the development of the mathematical disciplines including astronomy. In the early medieval schools they were studied as part of the seven liberal arts and constituted one of the two major subdivisions of the system,

48. Cf. Kristeller, *Studies in Renaissance Thought and Letters,* pp. 495ff.; Kristeller in *Artes Liberales,* ed. J. Koch (Leyden and Cologne, 1959), pp. 84–90.

49. For Galen, see R. Durling (see note 16 above). For Hippocrates, see P. Kibre, "Hippocratic Writings in the Middle Ages," *Bulletin of the History of Medicine,* 18 (1945): 371–412 (who fails to indicate which writings attributed to Hippocrates were available before the fifteenth century and which were not).

the so-called quadrivium. The actual content of this instruction was extremely elementary, however, compared with the achievements of Greek antiquity; this fact is not surprising if we remember that the ancient Romans themselves had but a modest part, if any, in these achievements.[50]

The rise of mathematical and astronomical studies in the West is linked also with the translations of Greek and Arabic scientific writings made during the twelfth and thirteenth centuries. Building on these foundations, the medieval scientists absorbed Euclidean geometry, Arabic algebra, Ptolemaic astronomy, and at least part of Archimedian mechanics, making independent contributions, especially in the field of mechanics, as has been emphasized in recent studies.[51]

Yet, it appears certain that some of the most advanced Greek treatises on mathematics were translated only in the sixteenth century and that the same century witnessed the first marked advances beyond the ancients, such as the solution of cubic equations as well as the new astronomy of Copernicus, Tycho Brahe, and Kepler.

By the end of the sixteenth century, Galileo had taken the crucial step that was to be the foundation for early modern science, that is, the application of mathematical methods to the subject matter of physics, which up to that time had been treated as an integral part of Aristotelian philosophy. If we wish to insist that medieval scholars of the thirteenth and fourteenth centuries had anticipated some of these developments, a claim that has by no means been accepted by all competent students of the subject,[52] we should not blame the humanists for having delayed the progress of science for a hundred years, but rather study the much neglected

50. W. H. Stahl, *Roman Science* (Madison, Wis., 1962).
51. G. Sarton, *Introduction to the History of Science,* 3 vols. (Baltimore, Md., 1927–1948); M. Clagett, *The Science of Mechanics in the Middle Ages* (Madison, Wis., 1959).
52. A. Koyré, *Etudes Galiléennes,* 3 vols. (Paris, 1939); E. Rosen (see note 46 above). A. Maier also makes fewer claims than Duhem or others.

work of the mathematicians, astronomers, and Aristotelian physicists of the fifteenth century, especially in Italy. Obviously, they must have been the transmitters of fourteenth-century lore to the sixteenth century.[53]

We can merely mention the steady progress made in such fields as technology and geography since they are hardly connected with philosophy and depend largely upon practice and experience. In the case of geography, it is worth noting that the best Greek sources, Ptolemy and Strabo, were translated for the first time by fifteenth-century humanists.[54] These translations were extremely popular and they probably helped to develop the interest in travels and explorations which culminated in the discovery of the New World.

Before we proceed to the other sciences and to the Aristotelian philosophy of which they formed a part, we must discuss briefly the so-called pseudosciences, that is, the occult tradition. Long ridiculed as a monument of medieval superstition, these disciplines have now been recognized as close companions of the contemporary sciences. Whatever occasional opposition they met with was based on religious rather than scientific grounds.[55]

The development of the various disciplines, especially astrology, alchemy, and magic, was not identical. Intellectually, astrology was the most respectable and had its precedents in late antiquity, whereas alchemy and magic were more practical and depended largely on Arabic authorities. All these studies may have found

53. M. Clagett, *Giovanni Marliani and Late Medieval Physics* (New York, 1941); J. H. Randall, *The School of Padua and the Emergence of Modern Science* (Padua, 1961); Randall, *The Career of Philosophy: From the Middle Ages to the Enlightenment* (New York, 1962); Curtis Wilson, *William Heytesbury* (Madison, Wis., 1956).

54. D. Durand, "Tradition and Innovation in Fifteenth Century Italy," *Journal of the History of Ideas,* 4 (1943): 1–20. "Strabo," by A. Diller and P. O. Kristeller, in *Catalogus Translationum et Commentariorum* II, ed. P. O. Kristeller and E. F. Cranz (Washington, 1971), pp. 225–233.

55. See the monumental work by L. Thorndike, *A History of Magic and Experimental Science,* 8 vols. (New York, 1923–1958).

fertile soil in the early medieval habit of symbolical and allegorical thought, but they did not develop substantially until the twelfth century, when numerous treatises dealing with these subjects began to be translated from Arabic. Astrology was allied with astronomy and medicine and became an integral part of cosmology. Although it met opposition during the Middle Ages, as before and after, it received much public recognition and was even taught at various universities. Alchemy and magic never attained such academic status and catered more openly to the material ambitions of princes and private individuals.

During the Renaissance, the occult sciences met with occasional opposition from theologians and humanists rather than from scientists; but, on the whole, their influence and appeal continued and even increased in comparison with the previous period. The cosmology of many Renaissance Platonists and sixteenth-century philosophers of nature posited a universe animated by a world soul and held together by hidden forces of affinity, which the wise and properly trained scholar could detect and control.[56] Thus Arabian occult writings were as popular in many circles during the sixteenth century as they had ever been before.

It was only the physical science of the seventeenth and eighteenth centuries that gradually brought about a neat separation between genuine and false sciences and put an end to the fantastic cosmology of the Middle Ages and Renaissance. Since its disappearance from the realm of science, this cosmology has continued to exercise a nostalgic appeal and to lead a precarious existence in modern poetry and occultism, just as pagan gods and myths survived in the Christian Middle Ages and Renaissance after they had ceased to be the objects of actual religious belief and worship.[57]

56. D. P. Walker, *Spiritual and Demonic Magic from Ficino to Campanella* (London, 1958).

57. F. von Bezold, *Das Fortleben der antiken Goetter im mittelalterlichen Humanismus* (Bonn, 1922); J. Seznec, *La survivance des dieux antiques* (London, 1940), Engl. trans. by B. Sessions, *The Survival of the Pagan*

Returning from the occult to the genuine sciences, we encounter at the same time one of the two great philosophical traditions, Aristotelianism. For the study of physics as well as biology was pursued during the later Middle Ages as an integral part of Aristotelian philosophy, in the same manner as logic, ethics, or metaphysics.

The greatness of Aristotle as a philosopher was generally recognized throughout later antiquity, yet his most important systematic writings apparently remained unpublished for several centuries after his death. He left behind an organized school which flourished for a long period. His chief works were made the subject of detailed commentaries by members of this school and later by the Neoplatonists, who held Aristotle in great respect and tended to combine his teachings with those of Plato and of the Platonist tradition. Yet, it was only among the Arabs that Aristotle acquired predominant authority to the extent that other Greek philosophers were excluded. There he became known as "the philosopher."

From antiquity, the earlier Middle Ages had inherited Boethius' translations of the first two treatises of the *Organon* along with Porphyry's introduction to the *Categories*. This group of writings was called *Logica Vetus* and formed the basis of logical study and teaching until the end of the eleventh century. The bulk of Aristotle's writings, along with those of his Arabic commentators and several Greek commentators, was translated into Latin only during the twelfth and thirteenth centuries.[58] When the medieval univer-

---

Gods (New York, 1953); E. Wind, *Pagan Mysteries in the Renaissance* (New Haven, 1958).

58. *Aristoteles Latinus, Codices,* ed. G. Lacombe and others, 3 vols. (Rome, 1939– Bruges and Paris, 1961); L. Minio Paluello, "Jacobus Veneticus Graecus: Canonist and Translator of Aristotle," *Traditio,* 8 (1952): 265–304, and many other papers published by the same scholar in the *Rivista di filosofia neoscolastica* and elsewhere. Fundamental are still the chapters contributed by the late Mons. A. Pelzer to the first two volumes of M. De Wulf's *Histoire de la philosophie médiévale,* 6th ed., I (1934): 64–80 and II (1936): 25–58, of which the second is omitted in the English translation of Vols. I and II by E. C. Messenger (London, 1935–1938). Of

sities reached their full development during the thirteenth century, the works of Aristotle were adopted as standard textbooks for the philosophical disciplines. Philosophy was thus taught for the first time in the West as an independent discipline distinct from the liberal arts and theology; and it is no coincidence that the modern terms for several philosophical and scientific disciplines correspond to the titles of those works of Aristotle that were used as textbooks: physics, ethics, metaphysics.

Through these works of Aristotle, the West acquired not only a large body of specific problems and specific ideas, but also a developed terminology and a strict method of reasoning as well as a systematic and reasonably complete framework within which all relevant problems could be treated and discussed. The study of biology, and especially the great work done in physics during the thirteenth and fourteenth centuries was due, as we know, to students and interpreters of Aristotle. In many instances they departed from the text and doctrine of Aristotle and developed theories of their own, such as the *impetus* theory of projectile motion.[59] It is now widely agreed that the Paris Aristotelians of the fourteenth century took the first steps in the realm of physics that prepared the way for early modern science, although opinions differ much concerning the extent to which they anticipated the work of Galileo and Newton.[60] If Galileo was partly indebted to the work of the Aristotelian school, as he seems to have been, this was caused by the influence of the Aristotelian tradition which flourished at the Italian universities during the fifteenth and sixteenth centuries.[61] For the Italian Aristotelians of the Renaissance

Messenger's "definitive" translation only the first volume has appeared (New York, 1952).

59. A. Maier, *Zwei Grundprobleme der scholastischen Naturphilosophie,* 2d ed. (Rome, 1951).

60. See notes 46 and 52 above.

61. See note 53 above and also A. Koyré, *Etudes Galiléennes,* 3 vols. (Paris, 1939). For the influence of Buridan in Italy, see G. Federici Vescovini, "Su alcuni manoscritti di Buridano," *Rivista critica di storia della filosofia* 15 (1960): 413–427.

continued and developed the work of their French and English predecessors of the fourteenth century. Instead of blaming the humanists for their failure to contribute to physics (which would be like blaming historians, literary critics, or existentialist philosophers of our time for not promoting our contemporary progress in atomic physics or in technology), we should study the much neglected work of these contemporaries of the humanists who were professionally concerned with the study of physics. Only in this way will it be possible to understand the history of physics before Galileo and to evaluate the contributions made during the entire period.

On the other hand, the Renaissance did not merely witness a continuation of late medieval Aristotelianism. The humanists supplied new translations of Aristotle[62] and translated all Greek commentators of Aristotle, many of them for the first time.[63] Thus a tendency to emphasize the original, Greek Aristotle instead of his medieval Arabic and Latin translators and commentators developed.

Moreover, several waves of anti-Aristotelianism emerged, which tended to reduce Aristotle's authority although they were not immediately successful in overthrowing it. Many humanists attacked the Aristotelian tradition in natural philosophy in the name of man's moral concerns and literary scholarship. The Byzantine debate about the superiority of Plato and Aristotle had its repercussions in the West; and the rise of Platonism in the fifteenth century, though not necessarily anti-Aristotelian, no doubt had a limiting effect upon Aristotle's authority. Finally, in the sixteenth and early seventeenth century, the great philosophers of nature

62. Kristeller, *Studies,* pp. 339–342; J. Soudek, "The Genesis," and "Leonardo Bruni and His Public," see note 17 above. Much bibliographical and other material on the humanist translations of Aristotle has been collected by Prof. F. E. Cranz but not yet published.

63. For Alexander of Aphrodisias, see F. E. Cranz in *Catalogus Translationum et Commentariorum,* Vol. I, ed. Kristeller, pp. 77–135; Vol. II, ed. Kristeller and Cranz, pp. 411–422.

from Cardano and Telesio to Bruno and Campanella consistently opposed the authority and doctrine of Aristotle and attempted to develop new systems of the physical universe to replace that of Aristotle and his school.

Yet, it was Galileo alone who succeeded in placing physics on a firm new foundation which was mathematical and experimental in nature. With him, the Aristotelian tradition in physics came to an end, whatever his partial indebtedness to it may have been.[64] Although we cannot claim Galileo as a representative of the Renaissance, there is no doubt that his work was at least as much indebted to Renaissance thought as to medieval Aristotelianism and more specifically to new developments in mathematics and astronomy that occurred during the sixteenth century, and to the recently increased knowledge of Plato and Archimedes.[65]

Whereas in physics the end of the Renaissance brought about an anti-Aristotelian revolution, the effects of which are still felt to the present day, Aristotle's authority continued to prevail throughout the Renaissance and into the eighteenth century in the field of biology. This does not mean that the Renaissance acquired no new knowledge in this area. It is enough to remember the study of the hitherto unknown flora and fauna of the Western hemisphere, which was described with great care and attention. Yet, leading biologists tried to fit new facts into the familiar pattern of Aristotelian biology, rather than working out new concepts or theories.

After discussing those Aristotelian disciplines that have become independent sciences in modern times and are no longer treated as parts of philosophy, we must consider those subjects which are still considered the proper domain of philosophy. The field of logic,

64. E. Moody, "Galileo and Avempace," *Journal of the History of Ideas,* 12 (1951): 163–193, 375–422.
65. A. Koyré, *Etudes Galiléennes,* 3 vols. (Paris, 1939); E. Cassirer, *Das Erkenntnisproblem,* Vol. I, 3d ed. (Berlin, 1922); Cassirer, "Galileo's Platonism," in *Studies and Essays in the History of Science, Offered in Homage to George Sarton* (New York, 1946), pp. 276–297. For so-called Pythagorean influences, see also E. Frank, *Plato und die sogenannten Pythagoreer* (Halle, 1923).

with which we might suitably begin, was the only philosophical discipline of Greek origin that occupied a place in the scheme of the seven liberal arts, which dominated the school curriculum of the earlier Middle Ages. The study of logic was based on the *Logica Vetus,* to which we had occasion to refer, and hence retained a rather elementary character for a long time. Yet, the rise of early scholasticism, which began during the latter part of the eleventh century in the French cathedral schools, was largely due to an increased study of logic and the tendency to apply the more refined methods of logic to other learned disciplines, including theology. With the new translations of the twelfth century, the West acquired the more advanced logical writings of Aristotle, especially the *Prior* and *Posterior Analytics;* and thus a new foundation was laid for logical investigations during the subsequent period.

The thirteenth century saw also the beginnings of a further development beyond Aristotle in logic which was associated with the name of Peter of Spain: terminism.[66] In the fourteenth century advanced logical studies flourished especially in England. The work of what we might call the first Oxford school of logic consisted in a highly technical formal doctrine which centered on forms of inference, on fallacious arguments, and on interesting attempts to develop logical and even quantitative formulas for degrees of quality, and for the gradual transition from one qualitative stage to another.[67]

Usually overlooked is the fact that the Oxford tradition of late medieval logic enjoyed a tremendous vogue at the Italian univer-

66. J. P. Mullally, *The Summulae Logicales of Peter of Spain* (Notre Dame, Ind., 1945); I. M. Bochenski, *Formale Logik* (Freiburg and Munich, 1956), Engl. trans. by Ivo Thomas, *A History of Formal Logic* (Notre Dame, Ind., 1961); E. A. Moody, *Truth and Consequence in Mediaeval Logic* (Amsterdam, 1953); Ph. Boehner, *Medieval Logic* (Chicago, 1952).
67. Curtis Wilson, *William Heytesbury* (Madison, Wis., 1956). For the later repercussions of the medieval logical tradition see also Neal W. Gilbert, *Renaissance Concepts of Method* (New York, 1960).

sities between the late fourteenth and early sixteenth century, at a time when the English school had long ceased to be active. In this field, just as in physics, the Italian Aristotelians continued vigorously the work of their fourteenth century Northern predecessors, as university records, manuscripts, and early editions abundantly show. A more detailed study of these materials would aid us in understanding the impact which fourteenth century logic may have had on later developments in the field of logic and in other philosophical and scientific disciplines.

It would be wrong, however, to attribute all significant developments in Renaissance logic to the traditions of Aristotelian or terminist logic. Anti-Aristotelian tendencies were at work in this area no less than in natural philosophy. Even the humanist critique of Aristotelianism, which in the field of natural philosophy remained largely rhetorical and ineffective, led to influential if not entirely successful attempts at a radical reform and innovation of logic. Valla's treatise on dialectic was the first attempt of this kind to replace the logic of the Aristotelians and he had several followers and successors during the sixteenth century. One of them, Marius Nizolius, attracted the attention of Leibniz.[68] Another of these logical reformers, Peter Ramus, became the fountainhead of a school of logic that exercised wide influence down to the eighteenth century in a number of European countries and in early America.[69] Recently we have learned much about Ramus and his school; and it has become apparent that the main purpose of humanist reforms in logic was characteristically to simplify logic for the purposes of teaching and literary presentation and to relate or even subordinate it to the theory of rhetoric.

68. Mario Nizolio, *De veris principiis,* 2 vols., ed. Q. Breen (Rome, 1956).
69. Perry Miller, *The New England Mind,* 2 vols. (Cambridge, Mass., 1939–1953); W. J. Ong, *Ramus: Method and the Decay of Dialogue* (Cambridge, Mass., 1958); the same, *Ramus and Talon Inventory* (Cambridge, Mass., 1958); Neal W. Gilbert, *Renaissance Concepts of Method* (New York, 1960).

Whereas physics and logic were the main philosophical disciplines which every student supposedly studied, metaphysics and ethics were considered elective courses. Hence the impact of Aristotle's work in these fields was less extensive, a fact which is apt to surprise the modern student.

The tradition of Aristotle's metaphysics is closely linked with that of theology, as we might expect; but it would be wrong to consider the two disciplines identical. Since Aristotle himself applies the term theology to at least a portion of the subject matter of this work, it was easy to consider it as a treatise on "natural" theology. Yet, the study of Aristotelian metaphysics was not the same as the study of Christian theology on the basis of Peter Lombard's *Sentences* or of Thomas Aquinas' *Summa*. The difference lay in the subject matter as well as in the method and sources of knowledge. If we wish to show a link between Renaissance thought and the tradition of Aristotelian metaphysics, it is sufficient to point to some of the problems which continued to be discussed, or even acquired a greater importance. The discussion concerning the immortality of the soul, which occupied a central place in the thought of the later fifteenth and of the earlier sixteenth century, involved the interpretation of Aristotle as well as that of Plato; the controversy between Pomponazzi and his opponents illustrates this fact abundantly. The question of the superiority of the intellect and of the will was debated not only by the followers of St. Thomas and of Duns Scotus, but also by several humanists and by the Platonists of the Florentine Academy.[70] If the problems were the same, however, the solutions often differed, and even where solutions sound alike, significant differences exist in the arguments, in the emphasis given to various aspects of a problem, and in the reasons why a given problem is discussed or solved in a certain manner.

70. Kristeller, "A Thomist Critique of Marsilio Ficino's Theory of Will and Intellect," in *Harry Austryn Wolfson Jubilee Volume*, English Section Vol. II (Jerusalem, 1965), pp. 463–494; Kristeller, *Le Thomisme et la pensée italienne de la Renaissance* (Montreal, 1967), pp. 104–123.

The role of Aristotle's *Ethics* was more complex and perhaps more important. Prior to the thirteenth century, writings on moral subjects were largely influenced by Cicero, Seneca, and Boethius; by theological conceptions; and by popular codes of conduct such as those of chivalry. With the rise of scholasticism and of the universities during the thirteenth century, moral philosophy became a formal academic discipline for the first time in the West, based on Aristotle's *Nicomachean Ethics* and *Politics,* and to a lesser extent on his *Rhetoric* and the *Economics* attributed to him.

Since the humanists considered moral philosophy part of their domain, it was in this field, rather than in logic or physics, that the impact of humanism on philosophical thought was felt most immediately. Aristotle's *Ethics, Politics,* and *Economics* were the first of his writings for which the humanists supplied new translations;[71] and it was Bruni's version of the *Ethics* which kindled the first great debate about the relative merits of medieval and humanist translations—a debate in which modern historians have continued to take sides.[72] In his humanist garb, Aristotle as a moral philosopher found many adherents among Renaissance humanists, and it is no coincidence that the humanists continued to use Aristotle's *Ethics* as a textbook in their courses on moral philosophy. Yet, many of them preferred to combine Aristotle's ethical views with those of other ancient philosophers in an eclectic fashion whereas others opposed or ignored Aristotle's ethics in favor of Stoic, Epicurean, or other views.[73]

It has become apparent, I hope, that the influence of Aristotle was not a unified phenomenon. This influence, and the reaction

71. Cf. Leonardo Bruni Aretino, *Humanistisch-Philosophische Schriften,* ed. H. Baron (Leipzig and Berlin, 1928); E. Garin, "Le traduzioni umanistiche di Aristotele nel secolo XV," *Atti e Memorie dell'Accademia Fiorentina di Scienze Morali "La Colombaria,"* 16 (N.S. 2, 1947–1950): 55–104. Cf. the articles by J. Soudek cited above.

72. Kristeller, *Studies, pp.* 340–341.

73. Kristeller, "The Moral Thought of Renaissance Humanism," in *Renaissance Thought,* II: 20–68.

against it, differed greatly between the various philosophical and scientific disciplines which he treated in his various writings. It is interesting to point out that Aristotle's *Poetics* and *Rhetoric,* the former practically unknown during the Middle Ages, the latter largely treated as a work on moral philosophy, became prominent as textbooks of literary theory only during the sixteenth century.[74] They attained a position of authority in the later sixteenth and in the seventeenth century, that is, at the same time when his authority in physics came to be criticized and finally overthrown.

In trying to sum up the rather complex subject of Aristotle in the Renaissance, it might be best to state that the Aristotelian traditions of the later Middle Ages (especially in the fields of physics and of logic) were continued; that there developed, alongside with them, a new humanistic Aristotelianism that was based on new translations and had its center in ethics, rhetoric, and poetics; and finally, that there was a rising ride of anti-Aristotelianism which consisted of several quite different waves, scored a certain amount of success in logic, and gradually prepared the way for the destruction of Aristotelian physics in the seventeenth century.

Before I begin to speak of the other great philosophical tradition of Western thought, Platonism, I must admit that I am partial to it; and that the manner in which I understand and describe it, and even the historical importance I attach to it may be influenced by this partiality. Compared with the humanist or Aristotelian traditions, Platonism cannot be easily described in institutional terms. It is intangible in a sense, but no less important or pervasive.

In classical antiquity Plato's school was the one that had the longest span of life, and his writings were widely read at all times even outside the precincts of that school. The early Middle Ages

74. For the influence of Aristotle's *Poetics* in the sixteenth century, see B. Hathaway, *The Age of Criticism* (Ithaca, N.Y., 1962); and esp. B. Weinberg, *A History of Literary Criticism in the Italian Renaissance,* 2 vols. (Chicago, 1961). An analogous study for his *Rhetoric* has not yet been undertaken, as far as I know.

inherited from the Romans only a fragmentary translation of the *Timaeus*,[75] but a number of Latin writers transmitted in more or less precise form many teachings of Plato and his school: Cicero, Boethius, and above all, St. Augustine, who always spoke with respect of the Platonists and, in spite of his unquestioned piety and originality, was indebted to them for many of his philosophical ideas. The continuity of the Platonic tradition during the Middle Ages, which has been studied and emphasized extensively in recent years,[76] depends to a considerable extent, although not entirely, on the authority and influence of St. Augustine and his writings. This fact acquires additional significance if we remember that in early scholasticism, prior to the introduction of Aristotle, and outside the field of logic, St. Augustine was the chief source and inspiration of philosophical as well as of theological thought for the good reason that he was probably the greatest Latin philosopher of classical antiquity.

There were, however, other factors in addition to the influence of St. Augustine. The writings attributed to Dionysius the Areopagite, composed by a Christian mystic strongly influenced by Neoplatonism, had been repeatedly translated since the eighth century[77] and exercised a continuous influence on medieval theology. The greatest thinker of the Carolingian age, Johannes Scotus Eriugena, was a Neoplatonist in his general orientation. In the school of Chartres, where early scholasticism attained perhaps its highest development, cosmological speculation drew heavily on Plato's *Timaeus* and on his Latin commentator Calcidius. Moreover, the great wave of translations made in the twelfth and thirteenth centuries included at least two more works of Plato, the

75. *Timeus a Calcidio translatus commentarioque instructus,* ed. J. H. Waszink (*Plato Latinus,* ed. R. Klibansky, Vol. IV) (London, 1962).

76. R. Klibansky, *The Continuity of the Platonic Tradition during the Middle Ages* (London, 1939, repr. 1950); Kristeller, *Renaissance Thought,* ch. 3.

77. *Dionysiaca,* 2 vols. (Paris and Bruges, 1937) where all known Latin translations are given in parallel columns, along with the Greek text.

Phaedo and the *Meno,* and several works of Proclus, among them his important *Elements of Theology* and his commentary on Plato's *Parmenides* which incorporates part of Plato's text.[78]

During the thirteenth century, Augustinianism and Platonism receded before the rising tide of Aristotelianism. Yet, the Franciscan school of theology maintained at least in part an Augustinian orientation; and we have recently learned that even St. Thomas Aquinas not only preserved important elements of Augustinianism in his theology, but also borrowed several concepts of his philosophy from the newly translated works of Proclus.[79] In the early fourteenth century, a German Dominican composed a bulky commentary on Proclus' *Elements of Theology*[80]; Master Eckhart, another Dominican whose work inspired all later medieval currents of mysticism in Germany and the Low Countries, derived many of his basic ideas from Proclus and from the Areopagite.

It is against this background that we must understand the Platonism of Cusanus, Ficino, and other Renaissance Platonists. We know that Cusanus read Proclus and Dionysius[81]; and it is

---

78. *Corpus Platonicum Medii Aevi, Plato Latinus,* ed. R. Klibansky, 4 vols. (London, 1940–1962); Proclus, *The Elements of Theology,* ed. E. R. Dodds (Oxford, 1933, rev. 1963); Procli Diadochi *Tria Opuscula,* ed. H. Boese (Berlin, 1960), cf. my review in *The Journal of Philosophy,* 54 (1962): 74–78. "Procli Elementatio Theologica translata a Gulielmo de Moerbeke," ed. C. Vansteenkiste," *Tijdschrift voor Philosophie,* 13 (1951): 263–302, 491–531.

79. The Platonism of Aquinas is emphasized by A. Little (*The Platonic Heritage of Thomism* [Dublin, 1949]), and played down by R. J. Henle (*Saint Thomas and Platonism* [The Hague, 1956]). Yet, other studies have shown that Aquinas' doctrine of participation is influenced by Proclus and occupies a significant place in his thought. See L.-B. Geiger, *La participation dans la philosophie de S. Thomas d'Aquin* (Paris, 1942); C. Fabro, *La nozione metafisica di partecipazione secondo S. Tommaso d'Aquino* (Milan, 1939; 2d ed., Turin, 1950; 3d ed., Turin, 1963); Fabro, *Participation et causalité selon S. Thomas d'Aquin* (Louvain, 1961).

80. Proclus, ed. Dodds, p. xxxii; Klibansky, *The Continuity,* p. 28.

81. E. Vansteenberghe, *Le cardinal Nicolas de Cues* (Paris, 1920), esp. pp. 413–416 and 436–438. See also Nicolaus de Cusa, *De docta ignorantia,* ed. E. Hoffmann and R. Klibansky (Leipzig, 1932) for references given in the apparatus and in the index.

quite evident that the writings of St. Augustine were among Ficino's earliest and most important sources of inspiration.[82]

In spite of these tangible elements of continuity, we should not overlook the fact that Renaissance Platonism was in many ways different from medieval Platonism. Obviously, Renaissance thinkers gradually gained access to the entire body of Greek Platonist literature, especially all the works of Plato[83] and Plotinus; surely no one would contend that it makes no difference whether a Platonist has read all of Plato (and of Plotinus), or only few writings in addition to secondary accounts of his doctrine.

Secondly, the Renaissance Platonists were influenced in a complex manner by other intellectual currents which had not affected their medieval predecessors, for example, humanism and even scholastic Aristotelianism.[84]

Finally, the more important Renaissance Platonists were highly original thinkers, and must be judged on the basis of specific ideas as we find them expressed and developed in their writings. The fact that two thinkers are commonly labeled as Platonists, or that they read St. Augustine or some other Platonist source, is not sufficient if we wish to understand or describe their contribution to the history of philosophy. Thus Cusanus, Ficino and Pico, Patrizi and Bruno belong in a broad sense to the Platonic tradition; but in each of them this tradition assumes a different physiognomy. Time does not permit and my topic does not prompt me to discuss or even to mention the philosophical ideas of these thinkers, for which I must refer to the monographic literature on the subject of Renaissance Platonism.

I will, however, discuss one characteristic notion, since it seems

82. Kristeller, *Studies,* pp. 368–371.

83. E. Garin, "Ricerche sulle traduzioni di Platone nella prima metà del sec. XV," in *Medioevo e Rinascimento: Studi in onore di Bruno Nardi,* I (Florence, 1955): 339–374; Kristeller, ed., *Supplementum Ficinianum,* I (Florence, 1937): clvi–clvii.

84. Kristeller, *Studies,* pp. 38ff.; Kristeller, "Florentine Platonism and Its Relations with Humanism and Scholasticism," *Church History,* 8 (1939): 201–211.

to be relevant to the general problem underlying this lecture. For the very concept of a philosophical tradition, subject to many changes and variations but basically uniform and continuous, seems to have been formulated by Renaissance Platonists. The apocryphal writings composed during the later centuries of antiquity and attributed to such venerable authors as Hermes Trismegistus, Zoroaster, Orpheus, and Pythagoras contain many elements of Platonist thought which were absorbed quite naturally from the environment of Alexandria in which several of them originated.[85] The Neoplatonist Proclus and others accepted these attributions at their face value, treating the reputed authors as ancient sages who were the earliest witnesses of Platonic wisdom, prior to Plato himself, and hence his forerunners and sources. Marsilio Ficino borrowed this notion from Proclus and the Byzantine Platonists, developing it even further.[86] For him, the ancient sages were not only forerunners of Plato, but representatives of a venerable pagan philosophy and theology. He was also convinced that Platonic philosophy and theology, which had its basis in human reason, agreed fundamentally with Jewish and Christian religion and theology which rested on faith and revelation. Both traditions were equally old and lasting instruments of divine providence. In this manner, Ficino could consider himself a new link in a philosophical tradition that began with the ancient sages, culminated in Plato, and continued through the Platonic schools of antiquity, through St. Augustine and the medieval Arabic and Latin Platonists down to his own age.[87]

This notion became dear to many Platonists of the sixteenth century, and Ficino's translation of the *Corpus Hermeticum* attained for a while an authority and diffusion equal or even superior

85. A.-J. Festugière, *La révélation d'Hermès Trismégiste,* 4 vols. (Paris, 1950–1954); W. Kroll, *De oraculis Chaldaicis* (Breslau, 1894); H. Lewy, *Chaldaean Oracles and Theurgy* (Cairo, 1956).
86. Kristeller, *Il pensiero filosofico di Marsilio Ficino,* pp. 16–20.
87. See the letter to Martinus Uranius republished by R. Klibansky (*The Continuity,* pp. 45–47).

to that of his versions of Plato and of Plotinus.[88] It was in this context that Augùstinus Steuchus, a Catholic theologian of the sixteenth century strongly committed to the Platonic and pseudo-Platonic tradition in philosophy, coined the term *philosophia perennis* and adopted it for the title of his main work.[89]

I surely do not wish to endorse the fantastic views held by the Renaissance Platonists about Hermes Trismegistus and other ancient sages, but I would suggest that the Platonic tradition deserves the name of a *philosophia perennis* no less than other traditions which have since appropriated this title for themselves. However that may be, the name and its underlying conception show that Renaissance Platonism was fully conscious of being part of a tradition and clearly realized that this tradition, although of ancient origin, had had a more or less continuous life during the Middle Ages. We may thus say that the theme of our lecture receives an explicit confirmation through the historical interpreta-

88. Kristeller, *Studies,* p. 223.
89. Augustinus Steuchus, *De perenni philosophia,* in 10 books, with a preface to Paul III (Lyon, 1540; repr. Basel, 1542). The edition of 1552, cited in the catalogue of the Bibliothèque Nationale, does not exist; I examined the respective copy which has the shelf mark R 1782, and it turned out to be a copy of the 1542 edition, in which the Roman numeral X on the title page had been erased, making the year MDXLII appear as MD LII with a blank space. It is also included in the author's *Opera omnia* (Paris, 1578; Venice, 1591, 1601). In the edition of 1591 the text appears in Vol. III, f. 1–207v. Agostino Steuco was born in Gubbio ca. 1497 and died in Venice in 1548. In 1538 he was named Prefect of the Vatican Library and Bishop of Kisamos in Crete by Paul III. See *Enciclopedia Italiana,* 32 (Rome, 1936): 726 (by G. Riciotti); *Enciclopedia Cattolica,* 11 (Vatican City, 1953), cols. 1332–1333 (by G. Paparelli); Th. Freudenberger, *Augustinus Steuchus* (Reformationsgeschichtliche Studien und Texte, 64–65, Münster, 1935); A. S. Ebert, "Agostino Steuco und seine Philosophia perennis," *Philosophisches Jahrbuch,* 42 (1929): 342–356, 510–526; 43 (1930); 92–100; Julien Eymard d'Angers, "Epictète et Sénèque d'après le *De perenni philosophia* d'Augustin Steuco (1496–1549)," *Revue des Sciences Religieuses,* 35 (1961): 1–31; Charles B. Schmitt, "Perennial Philosophy: From Agostino Steuco to Leibniz," *Journal of the History of Ideas,* 27 (1966): 505–532; Schmitt, "Prisca Theologia e Philosophia Perennis: due temi del Rinascimento italiano e la loro fortuna," in *Il pensiero italiano del Rinascimento e il tempo nostro,* ed. G. Tarugi (Florence, 1970), pp. 211–236.

tion which the Renaissance Platonists gave of their own work and achievement.

In summary, we may say that during the Renaissance philosophical thought, without abandoning its theological connections, strengthened its link with the humanities, the sciences, and we may add, with literature and the arts, thus becoming increasingly secular in its outlook. The partial continuity of medieval traditions, the introduction of new sources and problems, and the gradually increasing quest for new solutions and original ideas makes the Renaissance an age of fermentation rather than an age of synthesis in philosophy. When philosophy and the physical sciences made a fresh start in the seventeenth century, they consciously abandoned both the traditions of the Middle Ages and the Renaissance. Yet, it could be easily shown that Renaissance philosophy shared in preparing the way for these changes and that its influence persisted in many areas of European thought until the eighteenth century.[90]

I hope that this summary and general talk may offer you an example of the continuity of a living tradition which is at the same time in a process of steady transformation. The thought of the Renaissance, considered as a whole, worked with some of the old material supplied to it by medieval thought but produced out of it something new and different which expressed its own insights and aspirations.

The concept of tradition which finds its expression in the idea of a *philosophia perennis* may still serve us as a model and guide. Our Western philosophical tradition has a long history; and I hope and believe that it has a future, although this future may be within

90. Matthias Meier, *Descartes und die Renaissance* (Münster, 1914); L. Blanchet, *Les antécédents historiques du "Je pense, donc je suis"* (Paris, 1920); J. Politella, *Platonism, Aristotelianism and Cabalism in the Philosophy of Leibniz* (Philadelphia, 1938); E. Cassirer, *Die platonische Renaissance in England und die Schule von Cambridge* (Leipzig, 1932); Engl. trans. by James Pettegrove, *The Platonic Renaissance in England* (New York, 1955).

the framework of a broader and more comprehensive world culture than we have yet known. This *philosophia perennis* will include not only the thought of the Middle Ages but also that of antiquity, the Renaissance, and the best of modern thought—not only because it happens to be there, but because it contains a core of truth which we cannot afford to lose. This *philosophia perennis,* in my view, will include Plato and Aristotle, St. Augustine and St. Thomas, Spinoza and Leibniz, Kant and Hegel, and many others. Some of their ideas may be refuted or forgotten, some of their writings may even be lost. For every idea in its material expression is subject to destruction, just as are works of art or cities. I am deeply distressed as anyone by the amount of destruction that we have experienced in our time or that we may face in the future. Yet, I take comfort in the thought that a valuable portion of past life and experience is preserved by history and by tradition. And if I may be allowed to conclude with a personal confession, I believe that nothing that once was can be completely undone. Even if destroyed in the material world and forgotten by men, it remains and will remain alive in the memory of an infinite being for which the past as well as the future is always present, and that is thus the greatest, the only true historian, and the keeper of the eternal tradition of which even our best human traditions, to use a Platonist phrase, are but shadows and images.

IV Appendix

7. History of Philosophy
and History of Ideas

The terms "history of philosophy" and "history of ideas" are frequently associated in current public and professional discussions, and many statements seem to suggest that the two terms are more or less synonymous, or that the former term, being old-fashioned, might well be replaced with the latter which for many ears appears to have a more fashionable and glamorous ring. Hence there arises the question what each of these terms really means, or what it should mean, and whether and to what extent it is justifiable to identify them with each other, to reduce the history of philosophy to the history of ideas, or to treat the former as a part or subdivision of the latter. I am not convinced that these questions can be answered through an appeal to ordinary usage since this usage is fluid and reflects at best the intellectual formulations and decisions of a remote or recent past. We may have reason to question the very validity of these decisions, and perhaps to suggest or make different decisions, and in case we are successful and obtain a reasonable amount of approval, these different decisions will be reflected in the ordinary usage of tomorrow, though not yet in that of today.

The attempt to discuss the meaning and relationship of the history of philosophy and the history of ideas is obviously difficult and hazardous. It involves not only the discussion of such complicated notions as history and philosophy (and idea), but also the shifting balance of the intellectual globe that includes the continents or territories denoted by those terms, and even of the academic globe that purports to be, with varying success, its faithful image. In a short paper, I cannot hope to present an original or adequate discussion of these difficult problems, but merely try to raise a few questions which to my knowledge have not received sufficient attention and may be of interest to philosophers and historians.

The history of philosophy has been of recurrent interest to philosophers and other scholars, especially in classical antiquity and again in the Renaissance period. It came to occupy a central place in European thought during the last century, especially in the wake of German idealism. Hegel recognized "history" as a major area of reality and of philosophical concern, as Vico and Herder had done before him, and thus left a living heritage not only to his followers down to Croce and Gentile, but also to Marx and his disciples, and to many other thinkers who cannot be called Hegelians. Hegel also did not conceive political history in isolation, but in his phenomenology and philosophy of the spirit came close to a concept of culture or civilization in which political and social institutions, religion and the arts, the sciences and philosophy are interrelated as manifestations of the same spirit and subject to the same "dialectical" laws of historical development. The vast progress which the historical disciplines made during the nineteenth and early twentieth centuries, not only in the field of political and economic history but in the history of languages and literatures, of the arts and religions, and of civilization in general was not influenced by Hegel's theories, but rather opposed to them. Yet, this vast body of knowledge and of learning imposed itself as an epistemological problem to such thinkers as Dilthey, Rickert, and Cassirer. Finally, Hegel considered philosophical thought itself as dialectical, that is, in a certain sense as historical, and thus foreshadowed not only Mannheim's sociology of knowledge, or Croce's claim that philosophy and history are identical, but also Heidegger's conception of historicity as a basic aspect or dimension of human thought and being. Within such a framework, the history of philosophy occupies a significant and even a central position for the philosopher since it elucidates the basic stages through which philosophical thinking passed before it reached its present situation. Any attempt to grasp or answer our present philosophical problems thus presupposes at least a general understanding of the historical developments which have prepared or produced these problems.

In the English-speaking world, both history and philosophy have recently followed an entirely different course which has affected their meaning and interrelation as well as the intellectual and academic status of the history of philosophy. Professional historians have mainly cultivated political and economic, social and institutional history. They have been more interested in the technical procedures of their craft than in its philosophical premises and implications. And many of them have been more concerned to emphasize and strengthen the ties of their discipline with the so-called social sciences (which are usually not historical) than with the so-called humanities (which usually are). Philosophers, on the other hand, have become increasingly indifferent, if not opposed, to historical studies. This does not apply to the pragmatist school which produced Herbert Schneider and John Herman Randall. Yet, most recent thinkers concerned with the analysis of language, with logic, or with the philosophy of science are convinced that the essential methods and insights of contemporary philosophy are of recent origin, and consider the history of philosophy as a collection of errors that is hardly of interest to the philosopher—less relevant, for example, than the history of science (although the latter seems to be equally full of errors). Perhaps a few exceptions are permitted for some great thinkers of the past, such as Plato or Aristotle, Spinoza or Leibniz, or for the history of those problems that now occupy the center of attention, as logic, the philosophy of science, or the philosophy of language.

An encouraging sign in recent years has been the increasing number of philosophical papers and studies which deal with the cognitive status, method, and "language" of history, and there is obviously a growing tendency among both philosophers and historians to reestablish the connection between their respective fields. However, I have the impression that most of these discussions are limited to such specific problems as the nature of historical explanation or the possibility of historical laws, problems which I am inclined to consider marginal, if not irrelevant, to the enterprise of the historian. Many of these papers also seem more concerned to apply to history, or to impose upon it, certain notions obtained in an entirely different context, rather than to understand the specific problems growing out of the work of the historian. Moreover, few, if any of these papers seem to pay any attention to the methods and cognitive status of such historical disciplines as the history of literature, of the arts, of science, of religion, or even of philosophy, although these subjects have been widely and successfully cultivated both in England and in the United States. On the other hand, I have the impression, which may be due to my ignorance, that these "intellectual" or "cultural" historians have paid even less attention than their confreres in political and economic history to the methodological and philosophical problems of their enterprise. I am acquainted with but one excellent specimen, and it is not really a philosophical disquisition, but rather an attempt to adjudicate the claims of rivaling schools of literary criticism. There is a variety of reasons for this absence of a philosophical theory of cultural or intellectual history. One factor is undoubtedly the lack of interest and sympathy on the part of most contemporary philosophers; another seems to be the curious limbo in which these cultural historians find themselves, linguistically as well as academically. In our colleges and universities, they are usually called "the humanities," and this term has respectable historical antecedents, to be sure, but in current language evokes a variety of pleasant, but ill-defined educational, aesthetic, and moral values rather than historical knowledge. Concealed behind this linguistic screen, they must escape the attention of those philosophers who have abandoned all other tools beside that of linguistic analysis. Moreover, in many humanistic disciplines and departments, antihistorical tendencies have been no less vigorous than in philosophy. Historians of literature have to compete as teachers with writers and critics, "new" or otherwise, historians of the arts with practicing artists and musicians, and even classical and medieval scholars are constantly urged to emphasize what is actual or "socially significant." Scholars are thus often tempted, or even forced, to conceal their historical interests (the term "scholarship" is actually in disrepute in many circles), and to spend more time on justifying their work to the public rather than on doing it, let alone on reflecting upon its method. And this situation tends to isolate the cultural historians in various disciplines from each other as well as from the historians commonly so called and from the philosophers.

Dissatisfaction with this state of affairs on the part of many humanistic scholars, of some historians and historically interested philosophers, has led to various attempts to establish some kind of cooperation between the various historical disciplines. Probably the most important of these has been "the history of ideas," launched by the philosopher Arthur Lovejoy through the example of his writings, through continuing discussions at Johns Hopkins University, and through the founding of the *Journal of the History of Ideas,* which for over twenty years has counted among its editors, contributors, and readers a large number of philosophers, historians, and humanistic scholars. In studying the varying usage and transformations of many terms and concepts in many areas and periods of human history, the *Journal* has found recognition for its work and for its subject matter, even among philosophers. On the other hand, the very name "history of ideas" seems to encourage some philosophers in the belief that the subject does not concern them, since ideas must not necessarily be philosophical or true. Thus the mere existence of the "history of ideas," a field in which historians of philosophy collaborate on equal terms with historians of literature and of other disciplines, tends to encourage philosophers to abandon the study of the history of philosophy in which many of them are not interested and for which they have not acquired the necessary linguistic and historical preparation and to relinquish the subject to other scholars. There are distinguished historians of philosophy among the philosophers of our time, to be sure, but it seems to be a fact that most recent contributions to the study of ancient philosophy have been made by classical scholars, whereas the study of medieval philosophy has been left largely to the theologians and to the historians of science, and that of Renaissance and early modern thought to the historians of literature and of the arts. The collaboration of scholars from these other disciplines is surely most welcome, and the more so, the less the philosophers themselves study the history of their own discipline. Yet, I am afraid some essential aspects of the history of philosophy are bound to be lost sight of when the subject is exclusively or primarily studied by scholars who lack an adequate training or central interest in philosophy and in its basic problems.

When we try to define the task of the historian of philosophy, we are immediately driven back to the notorious difficulty of defining philosophy itself. There have been almost as many definitions of philosophy as there are philosophies, and many thinkers have either refused to offer a definition or have formulated it in accordance with their views after having developed them on different grounds. In the course of its long history, philosophy has not only been defined and understood in a variety of ways, but it also has constantly changed its relations and connections with other important areas of knowledge or of human concern such as literature, the arts and religion, the sciences and the historical and scholarly disciplines. A history of philosophy that merely records the antecedents of one particular type of philosophy which happens to be endorsed by the author is obviously not sufficient, although such histories have often been written ever since the time of Aristotle and obviously have their own interest when the author and his position are significant in themselves. What the historian of philosophy should aim at, although he may not actually attain his end, is evidently a comprehensive study of all philosophical positions held in the past and also of all meanings which philosophy has had in the past, including many that are greatly different from the ones commonly held today. This task may seem so comprehensive and so vague that the history of philosophy might be thought to coincide with the entire history of human thought, including all scientific and religious, all literary, and even all popular thought. I do not believe that we have to go quite that far. I think we are entitled to set off philosophy in a specific and technical sense from the much broader area of human thought of which it is evidently a part. Philosophy in the specific sense may be defined as the attempt to think coherently and methodically about the whole of reality or experience, or about particular problems with conscious or at least implicit reference to this whole. By its method, it distinguishes itself from popular or literary thought and, by its intended universality, from the scientific or scholarly disciplines which are concerned with solving specific problems. In addition to its method and scope, Western philosophy is also defined by its tradition which goes back to the Greeks. We believe that, in spite of differences of opinions, of problems, and of terminology, there is a continuity in the history of Western philosophy from the early Greek philosophers to the present. Every philosopher is a part of this tradition, and is knowingly or unknowingly indebted at least to a part of this tradition. This tradition is held together by a common effort, by common problems and themes, and by common criteria of argument and of validity. It contains a large number of true insights, in addition to many errors, and even the errors may be understood as failures in a continuing effort to attain the truth. The history of philosophy does not show a steady accumulation of valid knowledge as the history of the sciences does, but it shares with it the mixture of truth and error, even in the work of the most distinguished thinkers, and the corresponding task of separating the two and of understanding them both. The history of philosophy is not a history of errors, as the positivists believe, nor a history of truth, as Hegel thought, but a history of the quest for a truth which is always attained but in parts, and always present as a goal even in the midst of errors. These are the assumptions which underlie the task of the history of philosophy and which I happen to share, though I know that they cannot be demonstrated or argued for: philosophy has a specific method and function, and a specific and continuous tradition, and the insights formulated within this tradition are partly true, and even where false, are understandable with reference to a truth at which all philosophers have been aiming. If a philosopher is willing to accept these assumptions, as I think he should, and to admit that the philosophical truth attained or aimed at by his predecessors is of intrinsic interest to him, then it follows that the study of the history of philosophy is a genuine part of the task of philosophy. Vice versa, on account of these assumptions, the philosopher can bring to the study of the history of philosophy something that no historian of literature or of another discipline can bring (unless he has also acquired a training and stake in philosophy), namely, an understanding of philosophical texts and opinions in terms of their relevance to philosophical enquiry. This does not mean that the historian of philosophy should ignore the relations between philosophy and other areas of human experience. He will have to pay attention to the religious, literary, and scientific influences to which philosophical thought was subject in various periods and to the impact philosophy had upon other aspects of a given period. Yet, he will concentrate on the central enterprise of the philosophical quest for truth as it is still being continued by philosophers in our time. Just as many strands of political and social history have been explored out of an interest in the past of some living institution, the history of Western philosophy is of genuine interest to the same extent to which we consider this philosophy as a living enterprise. If we are strongly interested in the meaning of our present language, we should pay attention to the recent or distant philosophical roots of many terms commonly employed. If we are trying to overcome certain current views which we consider to be false, we may find historical criticism a powerful weapon that will lay bare the sources and theories lying behind some present modes of speaking and of thinking.

Before we talk about the tasks which the advanced student of the history of philosophy should perform in his research, in his teaching and writing, a word should be said about his training. It should be obvious to every philosopher, but apparently it is not, that the only basis for any responsible treatment of the history of philosophy are the primary sources, that is, the writings of the philosophers, in the original languages in which they were composed. These are the texts and documents that constitute the evidence by which any assertion about the philosopher must be tested. Reliance on secondary sources is completely inadmissible, but it is frequent even in published papers. An extreme case was a paper on Aristotle presented at a professional meeting by a respected philosopher, in which the author argued that if Professor X in his remarks about Aristotle was right, Aristotle was a determinist. It apparently did not occur to the gentleman to look up the text of Aristotle, from which he could have easily learned that Aristotle was not a determinist. More widespread even than the reliance on secondary sources is the use of philosophical texts written in Greek, Latin, or other languages in English translations. Nobody will deny that a translation is an indispensable help for the layman, and a useful one for the specialist. Yet, the widely held opinion that a translation is a substitute for the original text, and that it really makes no difference whether I study a text in its original language or in a translation, is completely wrong and turns out to be a serious obstacle to studies in our field. No translation is without mistakes, and by using it without the original text, we put ourselves at the mercy of the translator's errors, and this may result in serious misunderstandings of the thought or intentions of the author. Yet, even when a translation is free of obvious errors, it will have to express only one out of several possible meanings which an obscure text may have, and it will blur the style and flavor, and above all, the terminology of the original. Anybody who has had occasion to compare the standard English translations of Aristotle with the Greek text will notice that it is quite impossible to retain in the translation a terminology corresponding to the original in its consistence and in the variety of its connotations. I have heard and read more than one clever discussion of Aristotelian doctrine that loses its foundation and becomes entirely irrelevant once we proceed from the translation used to the original text. There should be a general agreement that papers and studies which are not based on the original text would best be ignored by those who try to reach and express a responsible opinion on the subject. This means in practice that anybody who wants to get a hearing on ancient philosophy must read Greek, that a historian of medieval or early modern thought must read Latin, and that one cannot talk sense about modern continental philosophy without reading French, German, Italian, or Spanish. The same applies, of course, to more difficult and less widely known languages. Not everybody can read Russian or Arabic, Chinese or Sanskrit, but I cannot conceive of anybody writing serious papers or books on the philosophers who wrote in those languages unless he has first learned to master the languages. These are the necessary tools for the historian of philosophy, as mathematics is the tool of the logician, or physics of the philosopher of science.

Mastering these tools makes the difference between the competent expert and the slipshod amateur. If a student of philosophy refuses to learn the languages needed for the study of certain phases of its history, this does not mean that this study is philosophically irrelevant or uninteresting; it merely means that he excludes himself from an active participation in this study. In addition to a linguistic equipment, the historian of philosophy needs a certain amount of philological and scholarly training, for he is dealing with philosophical texts just as the classical scholar is dealing with ancient literary texts. The historian of philosophy may be obliged to perform philological tasks upon his texts if this has not been done for him by other scholars, and he surely will have to know enough about editorial technique and textual criticism to judge the work done by others and to make a critical use of his texts.

The job of the historian of philosophy extends all the way from the most detailed work on specific texts to the most comprehensive account covering the history of human thought, or at least of Western philosophy. His first task is to make the philosophical texts available. This may merely involve the careful reprinting of known writings. Even here it must be his concern to avoid errors of his own, and to correct those of previous editions. He may have to compare different texts found in earlier editions or in manuscripts, and to establish the correct text as it was written by the author, and sometimes to reconstruct the genesis of a text written and revised by the author in different stages. There are numerous instances where such textual decisions or emendations affect crucial points in the thought of an author. In many instances, the historian may be able to publish from manuscripts or rare editions additional writings of an author that had been unknown to previous scholars and that throw a new light on certain aspects of his thought, his development, or his sources and readings. When all or some of the writings of an important thinker have been lost, as in the case of many early Greek and Hellenistic thinkers, the historian must collect all citations and testimonies relating to these thinkers before he can attempt to reconstruct their thought or to assess their place in the historical development. I am acquainted with more than one paper on the history of ancient philosophy whose thesis can be easily overthrown by calling attention to an additional testimony which the historian failed to take into account. And there is a famous book on an ancient philosopher whose writings have been lost that remains completely dubious in its conclusions because the author failed to prepare his ground with a collection of the fragments.

Once the texts have been made available, the next step is to explain them, and a large amount of scholarly literature on ancient and other philosophers consists of commentaries on their writings. Also translations that have scholarly value belong in this category. The main task of a commentary is to clear up difficulties, and to explain apparent or real inconsistencies found between different passages of the same author. Once the text of an author has been elucidated, it is reasonable to sum up the main points and arguments of a given writing, and to pin down the author's opinions on the questions with which he is concerned. This is what the ancients called "doxography," and some of it is rightly in ill repute for its schematic nature. Yet, if it is done with care and understanding, it is still a necessary step in the procedure of the historian of philosophy. Normally the historian dealing with a given thinker will try to go beyond this rather elementary procedure. He will either study one particular problem or set of problems that seems to be of central significance for the respective philosopher or he will aim at a coherent interpretation of his entire thought, at least in its main features. In such a monograph, the historian cannot reproduce all details or cite all sentences of his texts, but he will select what he considers to be most important, try to discover the basic assumptions and insights of his author, and try to correlate his major views with them. Being interested in the thought of his author as a whole, he may also pay attention to his life, sources, and influence and thus try to establish his place in the broader history of philosophy.

If the historian of philosophy is not satisfied with writing a monograph or two, he may proceed along two different lines in attacking broader topics. He may either study the history of a particular philosophical problem or concept or term, and try to understand the different ways in which this problem was formulated, discussed, and solved by different thinkers at different times. Such an investigation might be broadened into a study of the history of an entire group of interrelated problems, or even of an entire philosophical discipline such as logic, ethics, or epistemology. Such a study, if carried far enough, may throw an unexpected light even on contemporary discussions, explain their origins and antecedents, or point up their limitations. The historian may also aim at a broader picture by trying to write the history of the thought of a whole school of philosophy, or of an entire period of the history of philosophy, or of Western philosophy as a whole. The immense amount of primary sources relevant to such a task will of course force the historian to select for direct attention only what he considers most important, and to rely for the rest on the studies of others.

We have tried to describe in an outline the tasks which the historian of philosophy has to face in his inquiry. In the last hundred and fifty years or so, great contributions have been made to this study both by philosophers and by other scholars, but much more work remains to be done. Unless this inquiry is steadily continued, there is not only the danger that our knowledge in an important discipline will cease to expand but that ground already gained may be lost again. I do not wish to assert that the ignorance of the history of philosophy will cause actual errors in philosophical thinking, for a modern thinker is free to set forth his views regardless of whether they repeat or contradict those of his predecessors. However, the lack of the historical dimension in much contemporary philosophizing gives it a certain air of triviality. I have heard an acclaimed philosopher present with great emphasis his latest discoveries, and it does not seem to have occurred to him or to the greater part of his audience that they happened to coincide with some elementary notions expounded by Aristotle. And what seems to me even worse, the limitation to certain fashionable contemporary problems tends to narrow the intellectual perspective, ignoring a variety of additional problems and of additional solutions that were offered in the past and are still potentially significant, and creating the false impression that there are no intellectual alternatives beside the comparatively few problems or positions that have been discussed in the most recent papers or volumes on philosophy. Philosophical thought thus loses its flexibility and is placed into a straitjacket from which at least some of us would like to see it liberated. The study of the history of philosophy seems to be one way, though probably not the only way, out of this impasse.

In pursuing his inquiry, the historian of philosophy faces a number of methodological difficulties which he shares in part with the historian of literature or of science and which are of great interest for the philosopher concerned with the problems of method and of knowledge, even though he may not choose to be directly engaged in historical inquiry. The historian of philosophy is interpreting texts and documents, as other historians do, but these texts are of a peculiar nature. It is easy to see that these texts represent his data, just as observations or experiments represent the data of the natural scientist. These data may be subject to different interpretations, but they are specific enough to make certain interpretations possible, and to exclude others. Moreover, interpretation is a kind of transformation, and we may very well ask what this transformation involves, and what are the criteria of validity that are followed in finding or defending an acceptable interpretation of a philosophical text or system. We may ask how far the interpreter is permitted to substitute his own terminology for that of the author without doing violence to the original meaning of his

thought. Conventional labels that used to be employed more frequently in the past than in current discussions, such as pantheism
or nominalism or Platonism and the like, have to be examined as
to the degree of their validity or usefulness, especially since the
historian obviously cannot dispense completely with terms of a
general nature not found in the writings he is discussing. The
question arises whether a historian of philosophy should aim at an
objective interpretation of the thinkers he is studying or at a critical analysis frankly dependent on his own philosophical assumptions and opinions. I am personally convinced that he should aim
at both, but that the two tasks should be kept separate and that the
objective interpretation should precede the critical discussion. Yet,
we may very well wonder whether an objective interpretation is
altogether possible or whether it can be neatly separated from the
subjective critique. I am enough of a Kantian to consider it important that complete objectivity should be maintained as a goal,
though we may never succeed in fully attaining it. And if it is
fashionable to stress "commitment" rather than truth, I wonder
why the primary commitment of the philosopher, and of the historian, should not be to truth, as it has always been, meaning that
the search for truth should steadily continue for the very reason
that truth has never been fully attained.

There is another even more fundamental problem that is posed
by the very existence of the history of philosophy and that has
been keenly felt by many thinkers ever since Hegel. Every past
philosophical thought obviously has a temporal element which is
"dated" and which is due to the personality of the thinker, to the
time in which he lived, and to the influences to which he was
exposed. On the other hand, the views of a past philosopher must
be interpreted, at least in part, as meaningful and intelligible, if not
as true, and in this respect every past thought has an eternal
dimension that detaches it from the accidental circumstances of
the time in which it was expressed and makes it present to the

interpreter who belongs to a different time and speaks a different language. If we deny this eternal element in philosophical thought, we retain of past thought nothing but its factual surface, and it loses any relevance that it might otherwise have for our own quest for truth. We are thus driven into the position of relativism or historical skepticism, a position which has also been called historicism and with which several distinguished historians and philosophers have struggled. The problem of historicism in this sense seems to me much more serious and meaningful than the question that has been recently debated under the same label, and once more the arbitrary limitation of terminology has served to block and to conceal certain fundamental problems rather than to solve them.

It is now time to state as briefly as possible what seems to be the accepted meaning of the history of ideas. This kind of inquiry has been admirably illustrated both in theory and practice by Arthur Lovejoy, and there have been a large number of books and papers published in the last twenty years or so that seem to fall under this description. The term "history of ideas" is of comparatively recent origin, if I am not mistaken. It is related to such expressions as intellectual history or history of thought, and perhaps is indebted to the German "Geistesgeschichte." The term "idea" has had a long history of its own from Plato through Locke to current thought and language. When we talk about the history of ideas, we presumably refer to concepts or terms that have a definable or describable meaning and are used in a linguistic context, and also to opinions or statements which include or presuppose those terms or concepts. It should be noted that the term "history of ideas" is not the equivalent of Geistesgeschichte, the main difference being the use of the plural "ideas," instead of the German "spirit." Whereas the German notion of "spirit," due to its Hegelian antecedents, suggests in each instance a complex system of thought within which any particular idea or term is determined and definable with reference to all others and to their common source, the English term "ideas" suggests an indeterminate plurality of particular thoughts or notions that are not related to each other by any definable logical or even historical connection. In other words, the American term is free from certain sytematic premises of its German counterpart and hence more flexible, but in turn it is at least in danger of losing a precise philosophical and even historical context. For this as well as for other reasons, another term such as history of thought might be preferable. Another ambiguity in the "history of ideas" consists in the fact that concepts as well as terms are a part of its subject matter. At the hands of a master such as Lovejoy, the complicated interplay between thoughts and words would receive adequate attention, but less skillful practitioners are tempted to forget (and certain contemporary modes of thinking would encourage this oblivion) that thoughts and words, ideas and terms are related but not identical. It is possible for the same idea to reappear under a different name, and for the same name to acquire completely different connotations. The historian of the "idea" of rhetoric might be led to believe that this idea has vanished since the late eighteenth century because the term has become unpopular with most writers and a use of dictionaries or indices would not always tell him that the same idea, though somewhat transformed, continues or reappears under such different names as English style or literary criticism. Vice versa, key terms such as nature or "idea," reason or art, have undergone such radical transformations that it is often difficult to write a coherent history of their development.

Now the history of ideas has no doubt turned out to be an extremely fruitful and interesting field of inquiry, and it is greatly to be desired that philosophers and other scholars should continue to pursue it and to make contributions to it. Yet, when the question is asked whether the history of philosophy should be considered identical with, or a part of, the history of ideas, I am strongly inclined to answer it in the negative. I would gladly admit that the two fields of inquiry overlap and have certain topics and methods in common. That part of the history of philosophy which consists of the history of problems, concepts or terms as used by different philosophers at different times evidently belongs to the territory of the history of ideas. However, there is a large and important area which belongs to the history of philosophy, but not to the history of ideas—above all, the monographic treatment of the entire thought of a given philosopher, as well as the comprehensive account of the development of philosophy as a professional discipline during a shorter or longer period or through the course of its history. On the other hand, the history of ideas is not only cultivated by historians of literature, of the arts, of the sciences, and of religion, in addition to the historians of philosophy, but its very subject matter comprises not only the thoughts and ideas of professional philosophers, but also those less systematically or clearly expressed ideas which we find in literature and in art, in religious and in popular thought, and these latter ideas evidently fall outside the field of the history of philosophy as we have tried to define it. We may even say that the very same philosophical thoughts and ideas receive a different treatment from a historian of philosophy than from a historian of ideas if the latter is not at the same time also a historian of philosophy. The historian of philosophy will stress the relation of a given idea to the entire context of the thought of the philsopher who expresses it, and to that of his contemporaries, predecessors, and successors in the history of professional philosophy. A historian of ideas who does not have a primary concern with philosophy will treat the same ideas rather within the context of the surrounding nonphilosophical thought with which they may be more or less closely connected. I am especially dissatisfied with the treatment several aspects of Renaissance philosophy have received from historians of comparative literature who tend to misjudge the originality or significance of certain Renaissance thinkers because they ignore or misinterpret their sources in ancient or medieval philosophy. Moreover, a historian of ideas unconcerned with technical philosophy will be inclined to treat the ideas of past philosophers like those of other writers, as incidental opinions unrelated to the basic and continuing philosophical quest for truth, and as merely decorative elements of a historical pageant that can be enjoyed and described without being seriously or precisely understood. It is quite plausible for unhistorical or antihistorical philosophers to relegate the history of philosophy to the limbo of the history of ideas, but I hope it is evident from what I have said that in this way essential parts of the history of philosophy would be sacrificed, and even those parts that would be preserved as a subject matter would still be sacrificed as to their adequate treatment.

Although the history of philosophy and the history of ideas are overlapping, but not identical disciplines, I should like to maintain that the philosopher has a great stake in both of them. The study of the history of philosophy is really the business of the philosopher, as we have been trying to show, although he will welcome the collaboration of scholars from other disciplines provided that they have a minimum of philosophical training and interest. The history of ideas is less specifically the business of the philosopher, but philosophers and historians of philosophy have been taking a prominent part in this enquiry because it is intrinsically of great interest, and because the history of philosophy, though not identical with the history of ideas, is in many ways related to it, and the borderline between them is not always easily marked or observed. The study of the history of ideas is also useful for the philosopher because it brings him into contact and cooperation with those historical disciplines that are commonly called the humanities, such as the history of literature and of the arts. Moreover, if the philosopher takes seriously his concern with the humanities and with the history of ideas, he will pay greater attention than he has done so far to the philosophical problems inherent in the humanities as well as in history, and to the place which these areas of human knowledge and experience occupy, or should occupy, in the total scheme of our thought and civilization. In doing so, he will go a long way to add to his philosophical thinking an important dimension that genuinely belongs to it and that has been unjustly disregarded in much recent thought.

INDEX

Aegidius Romanus, 124 n
Aegidius Viterbiensis. *See* Giles
Aeneas of Gaza, 106
Agli, Antonio degli, 31
Alberti, L. B., 112, 127, 128
Albertus Magnus, 57, 129
Aldus Manutius, 79, 80
Aleria, bishop of. *See* Bussi
Alexander of Aphrodisias, 27, 30,
    81 n, 121 n, 142 n
Alexandre, C., 97 n
Alline, H., 93 n
Anastos, Milton V., 86 n
Antonio da Barga, 8
Apostolis, Michael, 100
Apuleius, 88–89, 102
Archambault, G., 131 n
Archimedes, 82, 83, 143
Arethas, Archbishop, 93
Argyropoulos, John, 76, 82, 102 n
Aristippus, Henricus, 90
Aristophanes, 74, 77, 83
Aristotelianism, 17, 143
Aristotle, 5, 36, 75, 140, 155, 158,
    164
    and Averroes, 30, 105
    and Barbaro, 77
    and Bessarion, 101, 102
    in Byzantium, 71, 93, 95
    Categories, 66, 140
    De anima, 30
    De interpretatione, 66, 81, 83
    Economics, 147
    and Ficino, 55, 106
    on immortality, 27, 29, 31, 146
    in Latin antiquity, 89–90
    and logic, 144
    on metaphysics, 146
    in Middle Ages, 91
    and moral philosophy, 147–148
    Nicomachean Ethics, 77, 147
    Organon, 89, 90, 140
    and Pico, 107
    and Plato, 86, 86 n, 142
    and Platonism, 103, 149
    and Plethon, 98, 99, 100
    Poetics, 148

Aristotle (*continued*)
    Politics, 77, 147
    and Pomponazzi, 18, 19, 40, 48
    Prior and Posterior Analytics, 144
    in Renaissance, 143
    Rhetoric, 124, 147, 148
    and Steuco, 60
    translations of, 69, 81, 82, 83, 122,
        142
    and Trapezuntius, 101
    and truth, 46, 47
    in universities, 141
Arnim, H. von, 134 n
Athanasius of Constantinople, 103–
    104
Augustinus, 5, 7, 72, 155
    and Bessarion, 101
    in Byzantium, 96
    Confessions, 6
    and Cusanus, 103
    and Ficino, 32, 151
    and Greek philosophy, 128 n
    immortality, 28, 29, 31, 34
    natural law, 134
    and Platonism, 89, 149, 151
    preexistence, 35
    and Renaissance, 115, 118
Aurelius, Marcus, 66
Aurispa, Johannes, 74
Averroes
    and Aristotle, 30 n
    and double truth theory, 46, 47
    and Ficino, 105
    on immortality, 30
    and Pico, 56, 57
    and Plethon, 98 n
    and Pomponazzi, 39, 40, 41
Avicenna, 57

Bacon, Francis
    and Ficino, 19
    on man and nature, 10 n
Badawi, A., 69 n
Bainton, R. H., 130 n
Balbo, Pietro, 104
Baldwin, Charles S., 118 n, 123 n,
    125 n

72 73 74 75   12 11 10 9 8 7 6 5 4 3 2 1